your
NINE-YEAR-
OLD

Books from the Gesell Institute of Human Development

YOUR ONE-YEAR-OLD
Ames, Ilg, and Haber

YOUR TWO-YEAR-OLD
Ames and Ilg

YOUR THREE-YEAR-OLD
Ames and Ilg

YOUR FOUR-YEAR-OLD
Ames and Ilg

YOUR FIVE-YEAR-OLD
Ames and Ilg

YOUR SIX-YEAR-OLD
Ames and Ilg

YOUR SEVEN-YEAR-OLD
Ames and Haber

YOUR EIGHT-YEAR-OLD
Ames and Haber

YOUR NINE-YEAR-OLD
Ames and Haber

YOUR TEN- TO FOURTEEN-YEAR-OLD
Ames, Ilg, and Baker

your
NINE-YEAR-
OLD

Thoughtful and Mysterious

by Louise Bates Ames, Ph.D.
and Carol Chase Haber
Gesell Institute of Human Behavior

Illustrated with photographs by Betty David

Delta

A DELTA BOOK

Published by
Dell Publishing
a division of
Bantam Doubleday Dell Publishing Group, Inc.
1540 Broadway
New York, New York 10036

To Dr. Frances L. Ilg,
whose insights and enthusiasms
still influence and inspire us

CONTENTS

your
NINE-YEAR-
OLD

chapter one
CHARACTERISTICS
OF THE AGE

Nine is an intriguing age but one that is a little hard to pin down. This may be because so much of the Nine-year-old child's behavior is uneven and unexpected. Thus in making designs the child of this age characteristically makes a very small design OR a very large one. Other behaviors are equally unpredictable. Whatever may be said of the child, the exact opposite might be true on another day. This can be confusing to the adult and, we presume, also to the child himself.

Perhaps the outstanding characteristic of the Nine-year-old is the fact that the child is emerging from his long, strong preoccupation with his mother (or other caretaking parent). Whereas at Eight he could not get enough of Mother, now he seems often almost to resent her presence and her demands. Eight depended on, or at least related strongly and warmly to, his mother (and for that matter to other adults). Nine is more independent, more self-motivated. He is a self-starter and once started wishes to continue in his own way, at his own time, in his own direction.

In fact, some Nines are so independent that they like to be "loose on the town" without being checked up on too closely. That is, they like to be allowed to play for a few hours without giving too specific information as to where they are going and what they are doing. Or to spend money that doesn't have to be accounted for. Nine may do best if

allowed considerable independence and if given considerable responsibility.

Eight is one of the more characteristically expansive ages.
The Eight-year-old is all over the place, speedy, sure. Nine
is more anxious, more withdrawn, less certain, less speedy.

Though he does not cover as much ground, at least not as
quickly, as he did a year earlier, he is still into everything.
His interests are so varied and so numerous that his days
are almost too full. Each afternoon is filled with some activity—music lessons, sports, Cub Scouts or Brownies, choir
practice—always something. He is driven by time but hates
to give up anything.

Nine takes himself and his occupations very seriously
and wants to do things just right. A new sign of his maturity is that he can interrupt himself (or be interrupted), take
a little side trip, and then return to his original occupation.
He can keep his mind on what he is doing even when
something interrupts. In fact, most Nines not only can finish a project—whether it is a book or a quarrel—but *need* to
finish it after they have been interrupted.

We have described Nine as an embroidery age. Thus
some children, at least some of the time, need to elaborate
on their productions and are not satisfied till they have put
in every last flourish or curlicue. They do this not just to
get praise, as may have been the case at Eight, but to satisfy
their own inner demands. In fact, in this as in other ways,
Nine is remarkably independent. It is as if the child at this
age is using a more delicate mechanism than just earlier. In
many situations a girl or boy makes more subtle and finer
responses, notes smaller details. Emotions are more subtle.
The child makes finer evaluations, notices tinier details—on
a test, over radio or television, in a newspaper. During a
recitation or even when reading he may make little, fiddling
movements.

Not prey to as many self-doubts as he felt at Eight, Nine
seems ready to tackle almost anything. This is an excellent
age for perfecting proficiency in the basic academic sub-

jects. The child is so much interested in perfecting his skills that he is not only willing but eager to do the same thing over and over, whether it is throwing darts or dividing by one digit. In fact, some Nines almost get dizzy from being so wound up in an activity. They make themselves see a thing through whether it is a five-mile hike, mowing a lawn, or making a transformer. Boys, especially, sometimes seem almost obsessed; they have a true sense of a goal and, when working against time, as in a speed test, their first query is "Did I make it?"

Completing a task is very important now, and Nine wants to know the scope and context of any new task before starting. Nines can do most anything they make up their minds to do; willpower is very strong. Children of this age can expend energy to make themselves do even hard and unpleasant things if they accept the task or idea and feel that they are doing it of their own accord.

Confronted with an unfamiliar task, the child of Nine may say "Hm!" and then look the situation over before beginning. Nines do not leap in recklessly as they might have done when just younger. They may actually verbalize "Let me think about this. I always have to think first." That is, girls and boys both like to plan, want to know where they are going before taking the first step.

However, Nines are not above complaining that something new is "too hard." They do know when things aren't being done right, whether by themselves or some other person. Thus they show considerable social criticism as well as self-criticism. Nine has a new awareness of self and of his own processes. The Nine-year-old girl or boy may say "That is just like me." As the child thinks, he may fixate on a point on the wall and tell you later that he wasn't really seeing the point, he was only looking at it to help him concentrate.

Both sexes show a realistic evaluation of self, of others, and of what others think about them. They will not accept a compliment if they feel they don't deserve it. To Nines, things are what they are. Numbers give them great satisfaction, because numbers give things concrete labels—you know where you are with them. Also, Nine wants to know the monetary value of a thing whether it is a dress, a football, a house, or even Father's salary. The child is also inordinately interested in knowing everybody's age. Nines may speak of their own poor memory disparagingly, but actually they tend to have rather a good memory for certain facts and figures.

Sturdy and capable as Nines sometimes seem, their emotions vary, as do other aspects of their behavior. Thus the child of this age is highly variable in emotional responses—now timid, now bold; now cheerful, now grumpy. Of course every age has its mood swings, but they seem particularly wide at this unpredictable age.

One of Nine's main problems may be that he worries and tends to complain. He may not merely refuse any task that he doesn't wish to do, or that seems too hard, or that he hasn't personally put his mind to, as when he was younger. Now the child gives some plausible excuse for not doing it. In fact, many of his physical complaints are related to some required task. If a girl has to practice the piano, her hands hurt. If a boy has to eat some food he dislikes, his jaw pains him. If either girl or boy has to do homework, the eyes hurt. Fortunately, one can usually ignore most of these complaints.

The typical Nine-year-old enjoys intellectual pursuits. He likes to make inventories and checklists; likes to classify and identify and order information. There is a factual interest in seriation and categories—the insignia of ranks of army and navy officers, flags of the United Nations, kinds of cars, kinds of airplanes.

Nine loves to collect. Not only quantity but quality is now important. And he likes to keep his collections in order. His success in collecting is in part due to his persistence and his desire to accomplish a goal. Reasonably well organized himself, he likes to keep his collections neat. Sometimes his mother does not appreciate his hoarding instinct and feels his fury when she throws out something he treasures or if she inadvertently interferes with any of his collections.

Boys and girls of this age now can show a reasonableness

and fairness in their estimates and expectations of other people. They no longer blame others, at least not as much as they used to. They want things to be run fairly, and they themselves try to be fair. The beginning of conscience is in the making. Nine lays great stress on who *started* any difficulty and is highly disappointed if the adult in charge (parent or teacher) does not agree with his evaluation of a troubled situation. He is willing to accept discipline if he considers it to be *fair.*

Nine loves to talk things over, especially with his friends. As children of this age are quieter and more sober than earlier, they love a good long talk-fest in which people, things, and situations are discussed. They talk about the present and the future.

Paradoxically, future interest in the opposite sex is foreshadowed at this age by intense disdain for and disgust with the opposite sex. Many boys still will have nothing to do with girls. Girls reciprocate with such statements as "Boys are loathsome creatures." Those who hate the opposite sex the most right now may be the very ones who will be the most strongly attracted to it a little later on.

At some of the earlier ages, there is in many respects great similarity from one child to another. Nine is one of the more individual ages. Though we can make general statements about this age, individual differences here are very great, which adds to the unpredictability of this very special age.

Emotionally, Nine has been described as responsible. Much of the time he does take responsibility for his own actions. And though not bursting with enthusiasm, as he may have been at Eight, he is willing to attack the new and difficult. Even though uncertain about the outcome, he is usually willing to try. Nine may sometimes be impatient and quick-tempered and may flare up in anger, but his anger tends to be short-lived. In general, he is quite the opposite of impatient. He thoughtfully plans not only individual activities but often his whole day. Persistence is his middle name, and once he has started a thing he very much wants to finish it, and finish it correctly. And he would like to have other people do things correctly too, though he is not quite as quick to criticize other people as he was at Eight.

Nine is a loyal and devoted friend who can even overlook small errors and mistakes on the part of others. The *idea* of friendship is important to him. If he feels that he has hurt somebody he likes, this hurts him as well.

Nine is rightly spoken of as "self-sufficient" and "on his own." He is independent. He thinks for himself, reasons things out. You can depend on him, and much of the time he can be trusted. He has a new capacity to set his mind on a task and to see it through.

Though Nine is to some extent an inwardized time of life, the child of this age does not pull way into himself as much as he did at Seven. He is thoughtful but as a rule not as morbid, moody, unhappy as earlier. He may complain, but not constantly. He withdraws just enough to look things over, to get ready for a running start, as it were. But some Nines are apprehensive about their ability to do what is expected of them. They often underrate themselves.

The child of this age does not feel impelled to boast and to attack as he did at Eight. Now he thinks in terms of fighting with his brain as well as with his body.

Nine both controls time and is controlled by it. He plans his day rather carefully. On the other hand, he is such a busy person, his interests are so varied, that he often lacks time to do all the things he wants to do. In his race with time he may set his alarm clock for very early in the morning so as to have time for extra activity.

His command of space is improving. Now he can go on errands, as to the doctor's office or to a music lesson, by himself, even though this may involve a somewhat complicated route by public transportation.

All in all, it is probably fair to say that there is a change for the better at Nine. Many of the earlier tangles with Mother smooth out. Boys and girls seem more independent, self-sufficient, rational, thoughtful, and self-controlled. Their increasing interest in intellectual pursuits can make them, when they have time for adults, interesting companions.

One of the reasons that we find Nine a little hard to pin

down is that individual personality characteristics of Nine-year-olds show up so very clearly. At certain ages children seem most influenced by the behavior age they have reached. Most Eight-year-olds, for instance, tend to be extremely active and outgoing; most Ten-year-olds are compliant, friendly, enjoyable. There are ages when children are so much alike that parents, reading our descriptions of the age, often remark, "Why, you could have been writing about my Susie."

But there are other ages when behavior seems more influenced by the child's own basic individuality than by the stage of maturity that he has reached. And so it is at Nine. There appear to be tremendous individual differences, seemingly more noticeable here than at many other ages. These occur with regard to almost any behavior one might select. Thus:

Some have a strong feeling for their family, others seem quite indifferent to family matters.

Some love money, some seem indifferent to it. Also some spend every cent they can get hold of, while others are real misers.

Some are good with their hands, some are awkward. Some excel at gross motor activities, especially sports. Others dislike sports, avoid them when possible, and are poor at them when they take part.

Some adore violence and blood and thunder in movies or on TV, others hate any sort of violence.

Some have small appetites, some eat anything. Some are good sleepers, others have a hard time getting to sleep and staying asleep.

There are even big differences as to speed of behavior. Some zip through any task or activity, others are true slowpokes.

Of course, such differences are seen at any age, but they seem especially conspicuous at Nine.

Another kind of individual difference has to do with style of growth. Many children go along evenly, hitting each stage of behavior at the more or less average time and behaving as we describe. Other children hit each stage more or less at the expected time, but rapidly and sketchily, never showing too strongly what we believe to be characteristic age behavior.

Some children, from infancy on, tend to shoot way ahead of themselves, giving suggestions of more mature behavior that they cannot maintain, so that they then fall back to or even below what might be expected at their age.

Some children can be described as spurt and plateau children. They cling overlong to young ways of behavior till parents and teachers despair, and then all of a sudden, almost overnight, they shoot ahead to what one had been hoping for or expecting.

Some children express the stages of equilibrium (see Figure 1) very strongly, and their behavior is not particularly upset or upsetting even at the difficult stages of disequilibrium.

There are, unfortunately, others who express strongly the stages of disequilibrium and hit only briefly the stages of equilibrium. As one mother complained of her preschooler, "You said he would be better when he was three. He was, but his good stage lasted for only about two weeks."

Some children, no matter what the age, tend to have difficulty in one area of living. Thus eating always gives them a problem, or sleeping, or making friends, or getting along in school. Others seem to find some new difficulty at each succeeding age.

Some children, whatever the age, perform rather evenly as to motor, adaptive, language, and personal-social behavior (the four fields of behavior we think of in the early years), and some are above their age in one field, below in another. Most psychologists test older children with two sets of individual tests—a battery of language tests and a battery of performance tests. Thus they end up with a verbal IQ and a performance IQ. When children are more or less evenly endowed in the different fields, things are probably easier for them, and for parents and teachers, because everyone knows what to expect.

As it is the language IQ that most people think of when they talk about a child's level of intelligence, if language is way ahead of other kinds of behavior we tend to expect more of the child than he or she may be able to perform. If the child with a high language IQ who may be weak in other areas fails at any given task, adults may say, "He could do it if he wanted to." Asked how they know he could, they tend to respond, "Because he has such a high IQ."

It is important to keep in mind that much more than the IQ goes to school. The child who is verbally gifted may be weak in other areas, and the child who does not have a high IQ may have other equally important attributes.

Figure 2, which illustrates what we have found to be typical alternation from year to year of stages of inwardized and outwardized behavior, puts the Nine-year-old clearly on the side of inwardization. Your typical Eight-year-old, whom we customarily describe as expansive, speedy, and evaluative, is definitely outgoing. As compared to his just-earlier self, Nine is pulling in and also pulling away, especially away from a close relationship with his mother or other adults in authority.

We have long sought confirmation of our observation that a child's behavior seems to swing alternately between stages of equilibrium and disequilibrium and between stages of inwardized and outwardized behavior. This confirmation has been long in coming, but current research by Dr. Herman T. Epstein of Brandeis University[1] suggests that the brain grows in a series of spurts during which it becomes more receptive to teaching and learning. (Accord-

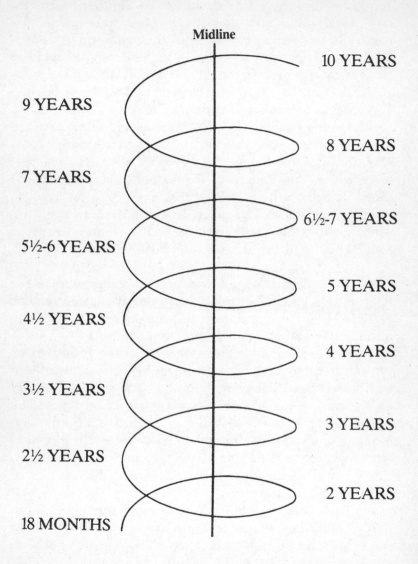

DISEQUILIBRIUM

EQUILIBRIUM

Midline

10 YEARS

9 YEARS

8 YEARS

7 YEARS

6½-7 YEARS

5½-6 YEARS

5 YEARS

4½ YEARS

4 YEARS

3½ YEARS

3 YEARS

2½ YEARS

2 YEARS

18 MONTHS

Figure 1
Alternation of Ages of Equilibrium and Disequilibrium

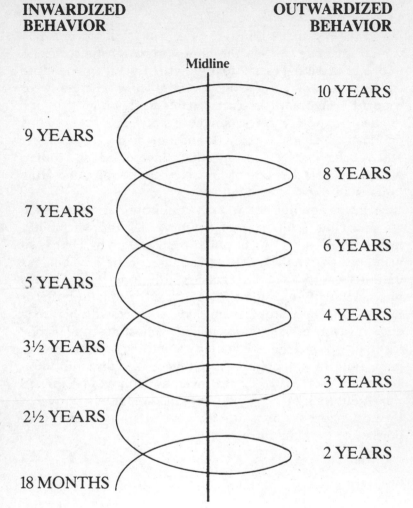

INWARDIZED BEHAVIOR

OUTWARDIZED BEHAVIOR

Midline

10 YEARS

9 YEARS

8 YEARS

7 YEARS

6 YEARS

5 YEARS

4 YEARS

3½ YEARS

3 YEARS

2½ YEARS

2 YEARS

18 MONTHS

Figure 2
Alternation of Ages of Inwardized and Outwardized Behavior

ing to his research, about 85 percent of children follow a similar schedule.) When the brain, primarily the cortex, is in one of these stages of rapid growth, myelin and dendrite connections are increasing to form new channels for thought. The brain is most teachable at this time.

There is quite a correspondence between Dr. Epstein's periods of little or no growth and our own ages or stages when behavior seems somewhat inwardized and quiet. Nine years of age is one of his quiescent periods, and Nine to us is an inwardized age.

So far as equilibrium and disequilibrium are concerned, we find Nine a bit hard to identify. His unpredictability makes it difficult for us to put our finger on him. He has so many positive characteristics that much of the time he does indeed seem to be in very good equilibrium. It may be his unpredictability that sometimes makes life so hard both for him and for those around him. This, coupled with his anxieties, his worries, his complaints, his almost neurotic inability to let go once he has started something, all combine to place him, in our opinion, slightly on the disequilibrium side of life (see Figure 1). However, as he moves on toward the equilibrium of Ten, good days may definitely outweigh the bad, and boys and girls may spend an increasing proportion of the time in the sun.

chapter two
THE CHILD
AND OTHERS

MOTHER–CHILD RELATIONS

One of the major changes that takes place at Nine years of age is that the child gradually detaches himself from his mother. At Eight he hung on her every word, absorbed her attention, wanted her constant company. In fact, as many mothers complain, the child of Eight tends to *haunt* his mother. He may not only prefer her company to that of his friends, he wants her *complete* attention. The relationship is deep and demanding.

Now at Nine most of the earlier embroilment has disappeared. The child not only no longer haunts his mother. He often does not really seem much interested in either her company or her conversation. Boys and girls are growing up. There is even less arguing back. At Eight it seemed as if the child preferred even negative attention, even angry dialogue, to no attention at all. At Nine this need is no longer present. In fact, if the child of this age does not want to comply, he or she no longer stays and argues but merely withdraws, emotionally if not physically. He is so independent, no longer tuned in to every nuance of Mother's voice or expression, that he may actually not hear what she is saying.

Children of Nine are often described as "in a fog," "in a daze," "in a cloud," so busy with their own activities that often they seem entirely unaware of what Mother is saying.

She may describe her child as being "in another world." He often seems to feel no personal resentment against her for making a demand even when it is something he doesn't want to do. He more or less ignores her unless the request makes sense to him. However, some boys, though still affectionate at times, are often sulky and fault-finding with their mother. Some are even bold and rude. And some even make very special efforts *to put things over* on her.

Boys, especially, react negatively to their mother's demands that they be neat and clean, to such an extent that many mothers find it saves time and energy to put a little less stress on cleanliness than they themselves feel necessary.

Nine does make a few demands of his or her mother as to how she herself should behave and how she should respond, but these are much more reasonable and less arbitrary and exacting than they were a year earlier. Nine is less disappointed now if Mother does not entirely come up to his expectations. Certainly the child has fewer notions about what she ought to do and say and how she should look and feel, and about what she is probably thinking about him than he did at Eight.

Until a mother realizes and accepts her child's newfound independence she is apt to handle it with too heavy a hand. Used to a total demand on her time and attention, she may find it disconcerting and even disappointing when all of a sudden her child turns away from her. If it has been their custom to do certain things together, she may find it deflating when son or daughter mumbles, "I'm going with Bobby" (or Betty, as the case may be).

Until she has had time to adjust to her new role, an unwary mother may find that she is coming down hard with specific demands. Most mothers are really pleased and relieved at their child's change in attitude, once they become used to it—it is just sometimes a little disconcerting to be so suddenly demoted. Often, almost without realizing what she is doing, a mother may become extremely directive about what her child shall do. It is almost as if she is saying "You may not prefer my company but I can at least make you wear your sweater, or come straight home after the movie." Thus briefly, till both become used to the new relationship, Mother may be unnecessarily bossy, child tiresomely resistant.

This is a time for a mother to step back, draw a sigh of relief, appreciate her new freedom, and be glad that her child is growing out of the dependence and entanglement with her that actually she may have found trying a few short months earlier. The child's newfound independence can actually be a big plus, all around.

One of the specific things that gives Mother more freedom is that now she no longer has to be there the minute her child gets home from school. Most Nines can have a key and can take care of themselves for a short period of time. (For the sake of safety, however, as well as for the child's emotional security, preferably this period should be not more than an hour every afternoon. Nine is not yet old enough to baby-sit himself.)

FATHER–CHILD RELATIONS

As most children at Eight are nowhere near as entangled with their father as with their mother, the difference in relationship that comes at Nine is not as striking. But it is still there. Now with Father as with Mother, the child tends to be less involved, less demanding of time and attention. (In those cases where a father is a house husband or has custody of his children, an Eight-year-old might be as demanding of his father as most children are of their mother, with a subsequent easing off of entanglement and demands at Nine.)

There is in many a growing respect for Father and his work. Many are quite proud of their father's occupation. Many are proud of being their father's child.

Most are very sensitive to criticism from Father and

equally appreciative of praise. Boys, especially, often are entering a new relationship with their father based on shared interests. Those fathers who are not strongly interested in very young children may be becoming increasingly involved with Nines or older children. Many Nines are at their best with Father, sharing some activity that satisfies them both.

Although many Nines mind their father better than they do their mother (they are more likely to "hear" what he says), both sexes, with their increasing need for independence, tend to resent what they consider "bossing" from either parent.

Most "approve of" their father, except for specific small criticisms, such as that he drives too fast or too slowly, or that he smokes. (Nowadays most children are much more critical of smoking than of drinking, by either parent.)

In some families, father and son—or mother and daughter—establish what seems to be a sex-linked bond.

RELATIONS BETWEEN BOTH PARENTS AND CHILD

Some responses appear to be expressed equally toward both mother and father—that is, toward both parents or to any adults (even grandparents) who assume the parent role. Some of these are definite improvements. Others temporarily make life more difficult.

One thing that tends to make life harder for parents than it was just earlier is that they are having to build a new relationship with their child, to accept new roles. Up till now the adult has more or less had the upper hand, or at least has been on a different level from the child. Many of the problems that arise now have to do with this relationship, which in the past for all a child might rebel and resist, has nevertheless been a sort of basic given.

Now many question their parents' infallibility and omnipotence. Unless the adult is skillful, a conflict may develop between the adult code and the contemporary code. Some Nines are beginning seriously to question whether their parents' rules are right. There occurs at this age something like a developmental level of parental handling as well as a developmental level of child behavior. Unless the two levels are matched, or at least unless the levels adjust to each other, there are apt to be fireworks.

While some Nine-year-olds are much interested in their parents in relation to things they can do together, even at this early age there may be a slight withdrawal from the family circle. Also, Nines are much less interested than earlier in the parent-child relationship itself. Therefore it is important not to impose yourself on the child of this age. He wants and needs his maturity, his independence and his separateness, and these should be respected.

Nine-year-olds particularly object to conversations about "my son" or "my little girl." They also object to things they had enjoyed a little earlier, such as talk about when they were little children. They especially object to any feeling that they are being treated like a baby when in their own opinion they are so very grown up. This may apply to perfectly reasonable demands that they keep themselves neat and clean and sensibly clothed. They react very badly to any hint of patronizing or condescension. Some may even not want to be recognized by their parents in public, as at a school affair. (This distancing will, of course, become much greater as adolescence sets in.)

However, there are many good things about the child's increasing maturity and independence. As parents tell us, "He is increasingly reliable," "assumes more responsibility," "does the most wonderful things," "is a pleasure to have at the table." Many are reliable enough to have and use a key to let themselves into the house (even though, as mentioned, they should still not be left alone for long periods of time). Some can even give substantial help in preparing a meal. It should be noted that these spurts of mature behavior are not continuous. Most children do not hold up to their highest level of behavior with any consistency.

RELATIONS WITH SIBLINGS

At this quieter, more thoughtful age, many children get on much better with their siblings than they did at Eight. They may be nicely protective of younger siblings and proud of older ones.

Nine in general, in his quiet, thoughtful way, may actually be quite good with much younger siblings if he is made responsible for them. In such circumstances he can often be

extremely understanding, without the strictness and sternness he may have exhibited a year earlier.

Inevitably there may be considerable difficulty with siblings close in age. Nine may argue, fight verbally or physically, compete, accuse.

However, a very secure Nine-year-old may, at least part of the time, accept philosophically the fact that a sibling is being given a privilege or treat not available to him.

Friends are extremely important to the typical Nine-year-old. As will be the case increasingly later on, girls and boys may have somewhat less time for siblings than earlier and thus may get into a little less trouble than earlier.

In the presence of contemporaries, Nine-year-olds may be much embarrassed or disgusted by the behavior of siblings and may feel that their parents should make them behave better than they do.

Nine is a strong age for interest in fairness. The child of this age may want to be sure that everything (blame included) is distributed fairly and so may be unduly upset if he feels he is being blamed for something not his fault. He is especially interested in "who started it."

Nine-year-olds may on occasion show real loyalty to a sibling who may be in trouble, standing up for that child when the occasion demands.

Nines may play quite nicely with a sibling of Ten much of the time, but fighting and bickering are common; wrestling if the two are boys; and much name-calling in any event.

Many have trouble with Elevens, since Elevens have trouble with almost anybody. And even at Twelve the older child is often much bothered by the mere existence of a Nine-year-old sibling. "He [the Nine-year-old] hits me but I'm not allowed to hit him" is a common complaint.

With a sibling of Thirteen or older, Nine gets on much better. Thirteen and Nine are in general somewhat quiet, withdrawn ages, and this may be one reason for this improvement in harmony. They just leave each other alone.

However, with siblings of Fourteen, things may take a turn for the worse. The older child may complain that Nine bothers him, annoys him, gets into his things. Discord may now amount more to general criticism of the Nine-year-old than to any excessive amount of squabbling or fighting.

If Nine's older siblings are Fifteen or Sixteen, regardless of how bad things may have been earlier, a parent may reasonably hope for a marked improvement—even a "very nice" relationship between the two.

RELATIONS WITH GRANDPARENTS

That teen-age time when many boys and girls become, briefly, somewhat distanced from grandparents is still far in the future. Most still are very enthusiastic about both grandmother and grandfather. The early love affair still continues. Grandparents are still proud of, much interested in, and very affectionate toward grandchildren. Grandchildren still look forward to times with their grandparents and still often feel that grandparents understand them better than anybody else.

They know that grandparents tend to be less critical, more permissive, and more admiring of them than their own parents are.

In talking about grandparents, children no longer describe them merely in terms of what they wear or how they wear their hair or that they wear glasses. Now the descriptions tend to be either in terms of specific things they do together, or even extend to broad generalizations. One boy told us of his grandfather: "He's a perfect grandfather. He brings us things and plays music with us and takes us places. He's a born leader. He gets things done. He would even make a good father." Others note that their grandfather tells good jokes.

Some girls still may say they like their grandmother because she makes good food and gives them things. But others have broadened out to such remarks as "I like her because she loves us" or "She is generous and understanding." "Nice" is an adjective used by many Nines in talking about grandparents. The relationship tends to be very smooth unless grandparents are members of the immediate household.

Most Nines greatly enjoy visiting their grandparents.

FAMILY RELATIONS

With the Nine-year-old, as with the child of any other age, behavior will be determined primarily by three factors: the child's own basic individuality, the level of development he has reached, and the environment that surrounds him. And of course at Nine in most cases his family still provides the chief part of this environment.

Clearly it must be quite different to be growing up in a two-parent family in which both parents are the child's own biological parents (whether or not the mother works outside the home) from what it is to grow up in a stepfamily. Even more deviant from what we used to think of as the norm is the situation where a child is being brought up, as a significant number are today, by a single parent.

Another major variable has to do with the number of children in the family. Regardless of whether it is favorable

or unfavorable, it is clearly quite a different matter to be an only child from what it is to be one of several siblings.

Within the family, the amount of attention paid to and the adaptation to a child's behaviors that are characteristic of any given age quite obviously vary with the kind of family in which he is growing up.

Say a child is a first, and wanted, child and has the privilege of growing up in the home of his two biological parents. Chances are that these parents will feel great interest (even though sometimes anxiety and/or despair) in stages he goes through as he matures. If the child is, say, a third or fourth child, his age changes will offer less fascination, and there will be less time to pay attention to and adapt to them.

Behavior will be as patterned, and as changing, as if he were a first child, but because there may well be less attention paid to it, it may express itself less vigorously. There is not much satisfaction for a Four-year-old to use a four-letter word or a profanity to a parent who has heard it all before and who really does not have time to dwell on it.

Even if the child is fortunate to be growing up in a home with two parents, if one of those is a stepparent, burdened with all the problems that many stepparents face, at least in the early years of a marriage, there may definitely be less attention paid to a "stage" than if both parents were the child's own.

Moving even farther away from what we have in the past considered the ideal family situation, we come to the single-parent family in which a single parent, often harried by lack of time and lack of money, is hard pressed to provide for a child the bare necessities of life, let alone attention to the special needs of each special age.

How does such a less privileged situation affect a typical Nine-year-old? Because a large part of the growth task of this age is to pull free from parental dominance and to establish one's own free spirit, less attention from a parent might seem to be all to the good. But we are by no means certain that this is actually so.

It is one thing to establish one's independence from a parent who has the time to be loving and caring and who still wishes to give attention. It may indeed be a somewhat lonely business to pull free from a parent who not only is not holding on, but who is not even noticing that you have left.

Conventionally part of any parent's role has been to be there as a sort of punching bag—a recipient of love and affection when the child has this to give, but someone to work *against* at the stages when the child feels the need to establish his independence.

Nine-year-olds, like children of other ages, undoubtedly benefit most when they are lucky enough to have parents who can notice and understand the stages they may be going through.

RELATIONS WITH FRIENDS

At Eight years of age the child's mother may be the center of his universe. Now it is more likely to be some special friend. And just as somewhat earlier the boy or girl quoted Mother, or the teacher, as *the* authority, now more likely a friend is quoted: "Billy says" or "Betty thinks." At any rate, friends' opinions tend to be more important to the Nine-year-old than parents' opinions.

Hero worship, at least on the part of boys, may be either for Father or for a same-age friend. As at Eight, many continue to have a "best" friend, though this may occur more with girls than with boys.

The Nine-year-old is loyal and devoted to his friends, admires them, is upset if a good friend is allegedly mistreated by parents or teacher, and protects his friends and may worry about some harm befalling them. He is especially eager to help if a good friend is in difficulty. Some, however, are less interested in the intimacy of the relationship, as they were at Eight, and are now more interested in the things they do together. Most get on rather well with playmates, even though there may be some quarreling and disagreement.

Boys and girls of this age have very positive likes and dislikes regarding other children, and may be quite assaultive, at least verbally, to a child they dislike. Some boys have considerable trouble with bullies of their own age or older. Fortunately, many are less susceptible to being teased and browbeaten than they were a year ago, though if things get really rough they may still look to an adult for help. (By Ten most can handle most social problems themselves.)

Children of this age tend to be interested in almost anything that concerns their friends—what TV programs they watch, how early they have to go to bed, or how much they have to help around the house. Girls enjoy spending the night with each other, either as a twosome or in some cases in slumber parties.

There is much good-natured roughhousing and wrestling among boys, who tend to dash about shouting. Girls are quieter. They giggle and whisper.

Nines tend to be strongly oriented to their group. They identify themselves with contemporaries and particularly with groups of contemporaries. They are working things out in relation to the group. Most like to please and to satisfy the adults in their lives, but it is contemporaries who are of primary importance to them. Their groupings or clubs tend to last somewhat longer and to have more structure. They may have a garden club, a scrap collection club, or a purely social club. Actually talking things over and planning what they are going to do often takes the place of any real activity. Secret clubs, for instance, may not go too much beyond planning a password, preparing for initiation, and assessing dues. Formal clubs under adult supervision, such as Cub Scouts or Brownies, tend to last longer.

At Nine as at other ages there are marked individual differences in the quantity and ease of friendships. Some children are so flexible and so sociable that if put down on a desert island (so to speak), they would find somebody to play with. Others seem extremely dependent on the whims of Fate. If there are other, friendly children in their own neighborhood, they make out nicely. But if the neighborhood lacks children, and/or if their school friends do not live nearby, they find it hard to go out of their way to make friends.

As with other behaviors, we relate need for friendships and ease in making friends to the child's physical type. Thus the angular, bony ectomorphic individual tends to be a person who is more likely to have a single close friend rather than many acquaintances. He is also one who makes

out very well, if friends are not available, with his own company and his own pursuits. Parents of such a child tend to worry about his lack of friends. They often feel that either they or their child has somehow failed. Often when

questioned they admit that they themselves have seldom been surrounded by friends and that they too really enjoy their own company.

In these early years, certainly even through high school, the most popular boys and girls tend to be the muscular, strongly built individuals who relate easily to other people and who are often looked up to and admired by less mature, less capable classmates. Their athletic prowess makes them popular. Their physical attractiveness makes other children admire them. And often they seem relatively mature socially. Such individuals like to be leaders and assume this role naturally and easily.

One further physical type that usually finds it easy to make friends is the round, plumpish endomorph. Such children love people, tend not to be critical or demanding, and are willing to follow the lead of others. This makes them comfortable companions. They tend to be genuinely fond of other people, admire their friends, and for the most part seem to have no wish to argue or to question or even to have their own way.

Parents may wish to step in, to whatever extent they are able, to encourage a Nine-year-old's friendships, if they are lacking. But it is important to accept, within reason, each child as he or she is. It is difficult enough for a child not to have friends without a parent pestering him or her to go out and do something about it.

chapter three
ROUTINES, HEALTH, AND TENSIONAL OUTLETS

EATING

The Nine-year-old typically has his appetite under better control than he did at Eight. He is more restrained and his appetite is better balanced. The good eaters have less tremendous appetites than they did just earlier, and the poorer eaters have improved. Even though he may not eat as much as he did a year earlier, Nine, however, may think about food more than he did formerly. Some even enjoy reading cookbooks or helping to prepare food. The minute most arrive home from school, their first thought may be about something to eat.

The child of this age is becoming increasingly ready to try new foods and will often even eat a little of foods he dislikes. Real hates, though, are still not accepted. Most children are eating well enough that their parents accept this, so there is generally much less fuss about the whole matter. For example, a mother may say quite calmly, "It's no use trying to get him to eat broccoli."

Most still prefer plain food, dislike sauces or casseroles or fat on meat, though many now will eat gravy. Boys and girls may also refuse a customary food if it is cooked in a new way. Most Nines are still not particularly adventurous eaters. Most look forward to dessert, which they eat with relish. Unfortunately, many also love junk foods.

Table manners continue to improve.

Nine is fairly deft with table implements. Many at this age cut well with knives, though a few continue to need help or tend to saw at their meat in their efforts to cut it. Fingers are rarely used to supplement forks or spoons. As at Eight, table manners are better away from home. But even at home, manners are improving and usually are not too bad. The child knows what is expected even though he does not always carry it out. A Nine-year-old is aware of bad table manners even though he may not be exercising good ones. He may even be aware enough of his own bad manners to keep an eye out for his father, to see if he is going to be reprimanded. Some actually do so well that they can be complimented on their manners. They chew more skillfully and are less likely to chew with their mouth open. They are also less likely to overload their fork, fiddle with food, or bolt their food. When asked, many say that nobody "mentions" their manners. Some can even combine talking, listening, and eating in reasonable proportion, though some still talk too much and still interrupt other people.

Now most Nines are better with their napkin than they used to be. Most at least start out with napkin in the lap, though admittedly it may still slide to the floor. But eating is so much better now that the napkin really is not needed quite as much as it used to be.

Although Nines' table manners are much better than they used to be—some are even said to add a positive note to a family meal—some children are still criticized by parents for their poor posture or for their open criticism of the food that is served.

Individual Differences: It is important for any parent, in adjusting his or her own expectations as to how much and how "well" a child should eat, to appreciate that there tend to be tremendous individual differences from one child to another in response to food. There are some—the round, plumpish boys and girls whom we call endomorphs—who love food. They live for it, are always eating, never can seem to get enough. Even when not eating they like to be doing something with their mouths, such as chewing gum. They like to think about food and to talk about it, are interested in cooking. They also find food comforting. When in difficulty or when things go wrong, they reach for a snack. Such boys and girls are almost never considered feeding problems. The difficulty, in fact, is not to get them to eat but to get them to curb their eating. These children often have serious weight problems, and thus their intake needs to be watched.

At the opposite extreme are the thin, angular children whom we call ectomorphs. Such children, thin but not underweight, often seem almost entirely uninterested in food. Parents of these children often worry a great deal, and often unnecessarily, that their children are not eating enough to keep them alive. The truth is that not only their feeding interests, but actually their feeding needs are very modest. So long as they seem healthy, and the pediatrician is not concerned about them, you will do best not to nag at them about their eating. Be sure they have a reasonably well balanced diet, but do not necessarily expect that this child will eat three "good" meals a day. In fact, try not to worry about how much or little your child eats. The less said about it, the better for all concerned.

In most instances quantity is not that important. Quality is something else again. One especially important individual difference with regard to food has to do with which foods a child can and cannot tolerate. Perhaps the majority of parents today try to be quite careful about their child's nourishment and make special efforts to see that their children, every day, have at least something from each of the four basic food groups: fruit and vegetables, carbohydrates, protein, and dairy products.

However, today not only pediatricians but also many parents are becoming increasingly sophisticated about the whole area of nutrition. We have become increasingly

aware that many children are highly allergic to certain foods. Most everyone recognizes the fact that a food or drink or even medication is bad for a child if it causes him to wheeze and sneeze, have difficulty breathing, break out in spots, or wet the bed. What has been recognized only recently (and this is still not accepted by everyone, including many medical schools) is that foods to which a child is allergic can also adversely affect behavior.

All too many children cannot tolerate such quite ordinary foods as milk, citrus fruits, cheese, chocolate, wheat products, and above all, sugar. Eating such foods may make them physically ill. Or even more subtle and dangerous, it can adversely affect their behavior. Though not everyone as yet agrees, it is generally believed that foods which the child's body cannot tolerate can cause hyperactivity, learning disabilities, and other undesirable behaviors.

And not only do some children not tolerate some foods, but many need other foods or food supplements (vitamins, minerals, other substances) that their bodies lack. Getting just the right balance—omitting harmful foods and fur nishing any food supplements needed—is a tricky business. But those parents who have achieved a good balance, either with the help of their physician or by their own trial and error, have found it well worthwhile in terms of improved behavior and a healthier as well as a happier child.

Books by Ben Feingold, Lendon Smith, Ray Wunderlich and Dwight K. Kalita, and Leo Galland, in our list of books for parents give helpful information about improving your own child's diet.

SLEEPING

Getting ready for bed is no longer a big problem for most, unless the child is sent to bed too early and feels that he or she does not have the privileges of other children. ("Nobody else has to go to bed this early.")

Nines still need to be reminded that it is bedtime, even when their television programs keep them posted on the time and when they know full well when bedtime is. Nine o'clock is the customary bedtime for boys and girls of this age.

Most go to bed with reasonable willingness, though some

prefer to read for a while once they are in bed. There is less need for being tucked in though some still do like to say their good nights. The majority are asleep by ten o'clock at the latest. If they do not want to turn off their light, or radio, by that time, a little parental pressure may be needed.

Night sleep is usually quiet though some have scary or worrisome dreams and a few may waken screaming from nightmares. If this happens, Nine-year-olds are usually quite easily quieted.

Many Nines wake spontaneously, around 7 A.M., after some nine hours of sleep. A few find that they control their waking best by setting an alarm clock. Some may even set the alarm early so that they will have time for their own preferred activities before breakfast. Some plan ahead for what they will do in the morning, such as reading, fooling around, watching television or even practicing a musical instrument.

Individual Differences: It is important for those parents who may worry that their boy or girl is getting too little sleep, or for those children who have a hard time getting to sleep, to realize that sleep needs and sleep habits vary widely from person to person. True, individual differences are probably greater in adults than in children. Some adults manage very comfortably on no more than five hours a night. Others need eight or nine and would enjoy even more. Children also vary greatly.

Other large differences occur in relation to the ease of getting to sleep. There are many children who are lucky enough to go to sleep almost the minute their heads hit the pillow. These tend to be the strongly built muscular children we label mesomorphs. Endomorphs too—those plump, round boys and girls who love their beds—often curl up and go to sleep without any great difficulty. It is the ectomorphs (the thin, angular children) who tend to have the most difficulty. These are the boys and girls who tend

to resist any change or transition. It is hard for them to go
to sleep and then hard for them to wake up in the morning.

Such children often lie awake for an hour or more before
they can manage to get to sleep. This would not do any
major harm except that they tend to worry about the fact
that they cannot get to sleep. Some solve the problem by
reading (either with or without parental permission). Others find that a radio can help fill in this wakeful period
pleasantly. In the mornings such children often need a little
warning ahead of time before they have to get out of bed.
They cannot leap out of bed, fully awake and ready for
action, as do their more strongly built brothers and sisters.

BATHING AND DRESSING

For most Nines, the bath is neither resisted nor especially
enjoyed. Three baths a week is about the average. Most are
able to take care of bathing by themselves but may do best
with a certain amount of supervision. They do appreciate
Mother's company at this time. Once in the tub most enjoy
soaking in the warm water, but there is usually less water
play and fooling around in the tub than there was a year
earlier.

Most Nines still need to be reminded to brush their teeth
and to do a good job of it. They may also have to be reminded to wash their hands before meals. But they usually
take this suggestion good-naturedly, as if they had been
planning to do it all along but had just forgotten.

Nines, like Eights, are quite capable not only of dressing
themselves but also of selecting what they consider clothing suitable for the weather and for the occasion. Most at
this age are better than just earlier at finishing up the loose
ends of dressing—buttoning buttons, zipping zippers, tuck-
ing in shirttails. Rips and tears are reported more faithfully
than they were at Eight, and some may even be quite insis-
tent about having things mended.

Nine-year-olds' natural instincts still tend to encourage

them to throw clothes around as they take them off at night, but most can now be taught to place them on a chair. Most are still not very consistent about putting dirty clothes in the hamper. In fact, most are not very proficient at judging whether clothes are dirty or not, and are likely to put on yesterday's clothes simply because they are handy. Boys, especially, often prefer old clothes to new.

Nines tend to be as negligent about hanging up outdoor clothing as indoor clothes. The minute they get home they are inclined to dump all their belongings on the nearest living-room chair or to fling them about. They usually respond well to being reminded to hang things up, but may respond even better to some device, such as having to pay a fine for each piece of clothing they have neglected to hang up.

Interest in purchase of clothes is increasing, though many are still reasonably content with what their mother brings home from the store, especially if it bears whatever may be the popular brand in their particular school or neighborhood.

HEALTH AND SOMATIC COMPLAINTS

On the whole, Nines enjoy rather excellent health. They continue to throw off colds rather quickly, for instance. However, children who have previously had ear, lung, or kidney complications may have a recurrence between the eighth and ninth year and may suffer a rather prolonged illness. There may also be an increased incidence of rheumatic fever, leg pains, and ear and throat discomforts.

Some at this age show marked fatigue and need to be protected from doing too much. When things are, in his opinion, "too hard," the Nine-year-old is very free with physical complaints. His eyes smart. His hands hurt. He has a stomachache.

These complaints nearly always represent real physical feelings of discomfort. Nevertheless, it is interesting to note how often they occur in relation to some disliked task. The child's eyes hurt when he is being tested or when he has to do homework. Hands hurt when he practices an instrument. His stomach aches if he has to sweep the floor or rake the yard. A girl or boy has to go to the bathroom as soon as it is time to do the dishes. All of these complaints should, of course, be respected within reason, but should nonetheless be recognized for what they are—Nine's way of meeting an unpleasant situation, not, generally, dangerous physical ailments.

However, parents should at least pay attention to the child's reporting of uncomfortable physical symptoms. When he says he gets tired from reading, it is something to look into. Or if he reports that he fatigues from color television but not from black and white, here again is a matter for investigation. The Nine-year-old is very much aware of inner symptoms that he feels when overexerted or strained.

He may say that he is "shaking all over" or that he "feels funny inside" or that something makes him "feel dizzy." Undoubtedly he is experiencing these symptoms. Listen to him but do not necessarily take him too seriously. Show him that you care, but discourage him from dwelling on these feelings. Nines tend to become quite apprehensive about their health. Don't ignore symptoms. Check into things but try not to share the child's apprehension. And be aware that some physical discomfort may be related to emotional factors, as with a boy who experienced severe stomach pains when his parents, rather thoughtlessly, killed one of his pet ducks and served it for dinner.

One aspect of health that is causing considerable concern is the fact that children seem sicker now than they used to be. In many families there occurs one health problem after another. Doctors are asking themselves why this is so.

There are undoubtedly many reasons, but among them are our increasingly polluted environment, windowless schools, the increased use of artificial colorings and flavorings, and the fact that much of the food available has been processed to the point that most of the good is taken out of it. A very special reason that may lie at the root of much illness is our increasing use of antibiotics.

This may seem strange, since obviously antibiotics can be useful or even life-saving, when they are needed. However, each time a person takes an antibiotic, he or she wipes out some of the friendly germs (bacteria) in the body and thus gives harmful bacteria (which make us ill) a chance to flourish.

Obviously, if your child develops a "strep throat," bacterial pneumonia, or meningitis, he'll need an antibiotic to help his immune system fight off the attacking bacteria. However, if he catches a cold or flu, antibiotics won't help, as these infections are caused by viruses. And taking antibiotics—especially repeatedly—promotes the excess growth of yeast and other harmful substances within the body.

So it is to be hoped that your doctor will advise you that, essential as antibiotics can be when they are really needed, you should go very easy on their use.

TENSIONAL OUTLETS

There tend to be many fewer tensional outlets at Nine than at Eight, or at least those that occur seem for the most part less conspicuous. A very few children still suck their thumbs, but this is decreasing even in the most persistent thumbsuckers. Those children who still depend on their thumbs usually respond well to parental reminding, or better yet to a dentist's warning.

Nines are likely to growl, mutter, sulk, or find fault if things don't go well. But in general, tensional outlets at this age are fewer than just earlier. And they involve less of the total body than they did at Eight. A Nine's most characteristic tensional release is through fine motor movements. He fiddles, picks at his cuticle or at a mosquito bite, drums on the table, runs his hand through his hair, shuffles his feet, or perhaps stamps his feet and jiggles his legs.

Boys let off steam by wrestling around. Girls are more likely to wander around the house, restless and moody. They fiddle around and can't seem to sit still. At school many restless Nines drum their fingers, draw in their breath or blow lips and cheeks, or hum, sing, whistle, whisper. Many grimace with failure or when a task seems too difficult.

There are very marked individual differences in types of tensional release at this age. Some Nines still make very large gestures, clapping one hand on their head. Others make very tiny gestures, as plucking at their eyebrows. Children of this age often seem more like their own individual selves, in their method of tensional release as in other matters, than like members of their age group.

Though this may seem an unduly early age for parents to start thinking about the more serious and what to most of us are more grown-up tensional outlets, unfortunately many of these are not too far away even for Nine-year-olds. Our own information gathered on over one thousand Ten-year-olds from all parts of the country is not encouraging. When asked if "any of the kids" their age whom they knew smoked, drank, or used drugs, 53 percent claimed to know kids who smoked, 36 percent said they had classmates who drank, and 13 percent said they knew other Ten-year-olds who used drugs.

Whether these children exaggerated or not, these findings suggest that nowadays such substance abuse is moving down to very young ages. In California boys and girls as young as Nine have founded a "Just Say No" Club to encourage other Nines not to use drugs. Reportedly these clubs are springing up all around the country. (And we recently heard a Four-year-old tell his grandmother, "If anybody offers me dope I'll just say 'No.' ") We have to face the fact that drugs are working their way down in the age scale, and as parents we should warn our children and protect them accordingly.

chapter four
DISCIPLINE

When many people think about the term discipline, they are really thinking about punishment. Admittedly a certain amount of punishing tends to be involved in any sort of discipline. Though some psychologists believe that we influence children most effectively by rewarding the good things they do and ignoring the bad, this is really not too practical in many households.

Most parents themselves have a certain emotional need to punish when things get totally out of hand. And in all likelihood a child who was never punished at home even when he or she behaved very badly would get a rather distorted view of what the real world was like.

There are, of course, numerous philosophies of discipline, and there are some households where discipline does not follow any particular philosophy but is chiefly "kiss and slap." In years long past grown-ups felt that children should be seen and not heard and that children had better mind "or else."

More recently in this country parents have been somewhat divided between so-called permissive and so-called authoritarian points of view. Permissive parents, strongly influenced by Freud, hesitated to punish children at all for fear of damaging their tender psyches. Such parents were labeled permissive because they permitted almost anything in the way of behavior, without punishing. Authoritative parents, on the other hand, maintained very strict discipline. They decided what their children should do and when they should do it, and punished any infraction of their rules or any failure to live up to their standards.

A third basic philosophy of discipline, our own, is called developmental discipline. It suggests to parents that they attempt to determine what is reasonable to expect of any given child, at any given age, in any given situation. If the child is *too young* to behave in some way that might be pleasing to them, he is not punished, or even reprimanded, for this inability. If on the other hand they have reason to believe that their child is mature enough to behave in some manner that they desire, but fails to do so, they consider that it is reasonable to punish, reprimand, or at least make some plan with the child as to how behavior could be improved.

In infancy it is relatively easy for most parents to respect their baby's immaturities. As Dr. Arnold Gesell used to point out, nobody punishes a baby for creeping instead of walking. And nowadays most people do not punish a Three-year-old for occasional toilet accidents. But when it comes to more "serious" behaviors, when inexperienced parents may mistakenly feel that the child could do better if he wanted to or really tried, many mothers and fathers do punish, we feel unjustly, for lapses from perfection that are really due to immaturity and not to sheer naughtiness. Understanding and respecting immaturity might prevent them from punishing.

Thus a parent who is practicing developmental discipline will not punish a Four-year-old for lying or swearing, will not punish a Six-year-old for saying "No, I won't," will not punish a Seven-year-old for not picking up his room. When behavior disappoints, such a parent will mention this disappointment, will urge the child to do better, will explain the ultimate goal—truthfulness, honesty, neatness, obedience. But he or she will be willing to wait.

Thus, clearly, the more one knows about the kinds of

behavior to be expected at any given age, the more realistic one's expectations will be. Most parents would be happy if their children reached the various aspects of desired behavior much sooner than most of them do, but some understanding of the customary timetable can help them to be patient.

Though many parents may not think of themselves as having a philosophy of discipline, most actually do, without perhaps verbalizing it. However, in most cases the kind of discipline that you as a mother or father practice is just something that works itself out as you go along, rather than something you plan formally. Mostly it evolves from the kind of person you are, from the way you live, from your relationship with your spouse, and from the way you feel about children in general and about your own children in particular.

If you are fortunate enough to have a comfortable, happy home life, chances are that your discipline will be reasonable, effective, and not too harsh. If you have an unhappy household, discipline may indeed be unreasonable, inconsistent, ineffective, and harsh. In fact, pediatrician Sanford Matthews, in his sympathetic book *Through the Motherhood Maze,* suggests, when mothers come to him distraught because their disciplining of their children is going badly, that these mothers concentrate on making their own lives more rewarding, rather than emphasizing merely their relationship with their child or children.

At any rate, whatever your personal philosophy and whatever the atmosphere in your own household may be, a solid understanding of what may be expected of a child of the same age as your own is bound to help you in disciplining because it will help you to make your demands and expectations reasonable.

Thus here is a summary of what one may, in general, expect of a more or less typical Nine-year-old with regard to such matters as the way the children respond to directions, how well they respond to reason, their sense of good and bad, the extent to which they blame and/or alibi, and their ethical sense in general.

RESPONSE TO DIRECTION, PUNISHMENT, AND PRAISE

In some children Nine may be an age of considerable rebellion against authority. Some Nines, however, merely rebel by withdrawing—they can look right through you as you give them a command. Or they rebel by complaining but actually do carry out your commands. And gradually the complaints, rebellions, and anxieties diminish as the Nine-year-old approaches the peaceful age of Ten.

Most at this age now can interrupt their own activity in response to a demand from an adult. Securing the child's attention may depend on his interest and willingness to carry out the request; and like his younger self, a Nine may wish to postpone whatever it is until later, and then forget. Thus Nines still need to be given rather detailed directions and, if they do not comply at once, may need to be reminded. In fact, most Nines are relatively easy to discipline but do require a good deal of reminding.

In general, there is much less arguing back than earlier. If the child does not like the directions you give he may look sulky, cross, or truculent, but if no issue is made of this he will usually obey.

Many prefer a reasonable appraisal of their work to praise, though praise is always welcome. And if they do resist, a threat of deprivation of some desired object or activity usually suffices to bring them back into line. Isolation works well with some. They may be "sore" at a punishment, calling it "a gyp," "not fair," or "just my hard luck," but most take criticism better than formerly, especially if it is carefully phrased. Nines tend to go to extremes. They may take authority on themselves to invite a friend home to lunch and then ask permission for some very small, unimportant thing.

In response to directions we have found that Six says: "I

won't." Seven says: "Do I have to?" Eight agrees: "If you insist." Nine complies: "All right."

RESPONSIVENESS TO REASON

Most Nines can make up their minds easily, and some can change an original decision in response to reason, though this does not hold for all issues.

SENSE OF GOOD AND BAD

There is now less concern than earlier about good and bad as such. Now most girls and boys seem to think in terms of right and wrong. They want to do things the right way and may be ashamed of being wrong. Many are able to say they are sorry when they do wrong. There is now great interest in fairness, especially fairness of parents and teachers. Nines are extremely concerned that any punishment they receive be fair. They also want other children to be fair.

Group standards are now more important to most Nines than parental standards, even though they realize that they have to respect the latter. They like to evaluate the behavior of other children: "He's a good (or poor) sport." They tend to be disgusted with others who do not live up to the standards of their group. Most are quite exacting not only of others but of themselves.

BLAMING AND ALIBIING

In keeping with their strong feelings about fairness, children of this age want any blame that may be given to be apportioned fairly. There is much interest in who started any difficulty. They try to explain their own behavior and may try to reason and explain their way out of any difficulty.

Some can accept blame and say "I did it and I'm sorry." They may even feel ashamed of their own wrongdoing, but are very upset if blamed for something they didn't do.

Most are very good at alibiing and in a tight spot may make up excuses for what they did wrong: "He was bothering me." And there is considerable taking it out on others. If hurt, they may kick the next person who comes along. On the other hand, many are quite ready with self-criticism: "I *would* do that!"

TRUTH AND HONESTY

Nines are usually quite truthful about their own misdeeds and lapses from virtue. Discipline is thus made easier, because at least parents do not have to go scurrying around trying to "get to the bottom" of things.

Though an exuberant Eight, for the most part honest and truthful, did sometimes expand into not entirely truthful exaggeration, and occasional pilfering of family money to buy things he needs, a Nine-year-old has improved considerably in both respects. A Nine-year-old might stray from the truth to protect a friend's lie. But even when he exaggerates he rapidly sets things right by saying "Oh, Mom, you know that isn't really true."

Nines rarely take things that don't belong to them, and if they do they may want to return them to set things right. They are now developing a sense of ethical standards and they mean to live up to them.

The words honesty and truth are now becoming a part of the child's own vocabulary. He may say, "I'll have to be honest." Certainly at least the rudiments of a conscience are developing.

PUNISHMENT

It is generally agreed that if discipline in a family is really good, there will be relatively little need for punishment. Nevertheless, it would be the rare household where no punishment at all is needed. Thus a few rules about punishment may be in order here. We quote a list of "dos" and "don'ts" from Joseph Procaccini and Mark W. Kiefaber's practical book, *P.L.U.S. Parenting: Take Charge of Your Family:*

1. DO fit the amount and type of punishment to the seriousness of the misbehavior.
2. DO punish immediately after the misbehavior.
3. DO make sure the child knows what is expected and knows he or she will be punished for misbehaving.
4. DO be consistent in punishing misbehavior.
5. DO administer punishment so that children feel bad enough about what they did wrong not to repeat it, but still feel good about themselves.
6. DO try to end all punishments on a positive note.
7. DO combine any form of punishment with a discussion of the problem and how to do better in the future.
8. DO try to let children face the natural consequences of their behavior instead of punishing, whenever possible.
9. DON'T deal with more than one misbehavior at a time.
10. DON'T punish a child when he or she is not aware of what is expected or is physically or psychologically incapable of behaving well.
11. DON'T use punishment to humiliate or intimidate a child.
12. DON'T punish your children without being absolutely sure they know why they are being punished.
13. DON'T play favorites with your children or be more lenient with one than with others.
14. DON'T strike your child if you're afraid you'll lose control.
15. DON'T continue to punish the child when the punishment should be over, even by unconsciously creating an unhappy atmosphere.

16. DON'T instigate actions or create an overall negative family climate conducive to problem behavior.[2]

These authors suggest that

In deciding on a course of action, a final alternative is to make a conscious decision to do nothing for the time being. Parents must learn to "choose their battles" in order to be successful. Sorting out which behavior problems to deal with is not an easy task; it often requires a great deal of introspection and objectivity. But it is a very important aspect of discipline. To ignore a problem behavior that should have been addressed allows a problem to continue and perhaps grow worse; to discipline a child for a misdeed that should have been ignored can create a climate of frustration and tension that could also lead to further problems. But how can parents tell the difference? When is it an appropriate decision to do nothing about a misbehavior?

There are stages in every child's life when rebellious, undisciplined behavior is common. Although parental discipline is essential in these periods, to deal with each and every incident would mean a constant battle between parent and child—not an atmosphere conducive to helping the child become more civilized overall. Since a lot of misbehavior in these periods stems from children's need to control themselves rather than to be controlled by their parents, it is a good idea to take a close look at the "house rules": Which ones have the highest priority, and are nonnegotiable? Which ones are less important for the time being? If you stick to your usual discipline plan for the important rules and bend a little for the less important ones, your family can become less of a battleground.[3]

To conclude this chapter on discipline, we'd like to quote further from Procaccini and Kiefaber. They ask parents to check to see how satisfied they are with their own parenting skills. For each of the questions in the following list, they suggest that you grade yourself. Give a 4 if you are very satisfied with the way you are handling the item in question, 3 if you are somewhat satisfied, 2 if you are somewhat dissatisfied, and 1 if you are very dissatisfied.

Here is the list:

DISCIPLINE SKILLS INVENTORY[4]

————— 1. I can keep in mind that my role in disciplining my child is to help him or her develop self-discipline.

————— 2. I am certain my child knows what behavior is expected.

————— 3. Family values are discussed with my child.

————— 4. Both parents are in agreement about family values and their priorities.

————— 5. I set a positive example for my child through my actions, not just my instructions.

————— 6. I can relate house rules, school rules, and society's laws to our family values.

————— 7. I am aware of what positive behavior to expect from someone my child's age.

————— 8. I am aware of what negative behavior to expect from someone my child's age.

————— 9. I view training as a large part of discipline.

—————10. I demonstrate behaviors I want my child to learn effectively.

—————11. I don't expect perfection right away when my child is learning something new.

—————12. I give honest positive feedback when it is deserved.

—————13. I give honest negative feedback when it is deserved.

—————14. I encourage my child to reward himself or herself for positive behavior.

—————15. I become aware of behavior problems quickly before they become serious problems.

—————16. I know what is happening with my child outside our home.

—————17. I can view my child's discipline problems in perspective without becoming overly upset.

—————18. I have a goal in mind whenever I discipline my child.

—————19. I am solution-oriented rather than problem-oriented.

—————20. I look at several alternatives before deciding how to discipline my child.

—————21. Whenever possible, I let my child face the natural consequences of his or her behavior.

—————22. I avoid pleading with or coaxing my child.

—————23. When I punish my child, I make sure he or she knows the reason for the punishment.

—————24. I never punish in order to humiliate or intimidate my child.

—————25. I punish my child immediately after a misbehavior.

—————26. I give my child prior warning about which behaviors will result in punishment.

—————27. I am consistent in the way I punish my child.

—————28. I avoid playing favorites with my children.

—————29. When scolding my child, I address behavior, not personality.

—————30. I am specific about what behavior the child is being punished for.

—————31. I combine any form of punishment with a discussion of what the child must do to avoid punishment next time.

—————32. I consider my child a partner in the venture of establishing control over his or her behavior.

—————33. I select a type and intensity of punishment that suits the misbehavior.

—————34. I avoid turning every possession, privilege, or event into a reward or punishment to control my child's behavior.

—————35. I choose my battles carefully in order to address the most important behavior problems.

According to these authors, there is no ideal or expected score. But if most of your evaluations of your effectiveness at disciplining are only 1 or 2, here's what you might do:

You might select two or three items that you wish to improve on right now and circle them. You can begin to develop a plan of action to help improve your own disciplining skills. After they are accomplished at a satisfactory level, select two or three more that you can work on. If this systematic approach is followed, improvements in disciplining will become evident to you and your family. All the way through the growth process, be sure to consider the attitudinal and emotional as well as behavioral aspects of the recommended principles and procedures.

The disciplining skills of mothers and fathers are a cornerstone of parentship. But effective discipline is not something imposed on a family in an arbitrary fashion. Rather, it is developed from the inside out. The essence of parental discipline is the ability to teach and motivate children to manage themselves.[5]

chapter five
SELF AND SEX

SELF

It may safely be said that most Nine-year-olds have a rather good feeling about themselves. Many parents have told us that their boy or girl at this age has shown a marked change for the better. Many of the earlier tangles seem to have straightened out. The child seems to feel much less tense than just earlier, more independent, more self-sufficient, more on his own, in better equilibrium than at Eight. Also the child may show sudden spurts of extremely good behavior. As one mother put it in describing her son, "He sometimes does the most wonderful things."

Your typical Nine-year-old tends to be, at least much of the time, very responsible. He can have a key and let himself into the house, get a (very simple) meal for himself, go into town alone, make modest purchases.

Much of the time Nines seem to feel very secure within themselves, very busy with their own personal concerns. They do not depend on other people quite as much as they used to.

And most Nines seem reasonably well satisfied with themselves and with their families. There is, in fact, a tendency for them to feel that anything of their own—Father or Mother's work or profession, their own belongings, their home, their city—is very special and very satisfactory.

Though most are mature enough to express a certain

amount of self-criticism—"I *would* do that!" "Oh, that's my poor memory!" "Well, you know me and my dirt"—they make this self-criticism rather matter-of-factly, as if that's just the way things are and there's not too much they can do about it.

Mothers do complain a little that because their Nine-year-old is so wrapped up in himself, sometimes it is almost as if he is in a daze, or they say that "things go over his head." This admittedly leads to a certain amount of carelessness, thoughtlessness, indifference, and irresponsibility. But once you get the child's attention, once you get through to them, as a rule Nines will try quite hard to do what is expected of them.

In general, parents find their Nine-year-olds to be dependable and trustworthy. If they say they have done something, as a rule they have indeed done it. Certainly a Nine-year-old has himself under better control than when he was Eight. He withdraws from his surroundings enough to gather up his sense of self and to put it to good use, but he does not retreat far into himself, as he did at Seven. He does not feel impelled to boast and to attack to protect himself as he did at Eight. Now he thinks in terms of fighting with his brain as well as with his body. For instance, he plans his time so that he can get off to school early enough to protect himself from being pestered on the way, if he is walking.

Nines have a new capacity to set their mind to a task and see it through. They are even ambitious in their demands of themselves. They want to succeed, not only in any single task but also in general.

A good relationship with others is important to a Nine-year-old, if he is going to be happy with himself. He is eager to please, wants to be liked, loves to be chosen. He will work for a favor, and he thrives on praise. This is the first year that many have themselves well enough in hand to do things in a spirit of service.

Nines are interested in themselves not only as they are

now but as they will be in the future. Boys and girls do a good deal of planning, often in great and often practical detail, for the immediate future or even the rather far-off time when they may be going to college, or even for what they may do as an adult. List-making, which is a favorite activity, is a part of this planning.

A Nine-year-old shows a great drive to succeed and to do things right. He may be extremely sensitive about any failure or about any criticism, real or implied or imagined. Nines may even on occasion burst into tears if they feel they have failed. They may also be quite self-conscious, both about their appearance and about their performance. We see many signs of the fact that, in his feelings about himself, the Nine-year-old is moving on toward the calm acceptance (of self and of others) that so many are able to express when they are Ten.

Many Nines are able to make a reasonably good evaluation of things they do well—as being a good athlete or playing some musical instrument. With typical thoughtfulness and niceness, a Nine may, if asked, tell you ways in which he or she is trying to be a better person: "I try to be kind," "I try to improve my temper," "I try to be calm."

One of our Nine-year-old friends reported, gratifyingly, "I have a good life, basically."

SEX

Nine years of age may be one of the low points for girl-boy interest. Dr. Gesell put it succinctly when he noted that

> In school the groups may include both boys and girls, but the spontaneous groupings outside of school are nearly always unilateral. Girls have their clubs in which some time is devoted to giggling and whispering, whereas boys indulge in roughhousing and wrestling. The boys have more trouble with bullies their own age or older. Birthday parties are usually by choice limited to one sex. Boys tease each other about girl friends. Girls tease each other about boyfriends. *Each sex cordially disdains the other.*[6]

That is true. For the most part girls play with other girls and boys play with other boys. There is, indeed, quite a lot of teasing about friends of the opposite sex, and some boy-girl attractions do exist, but as a rule they do not lead to much playing together. Some children always seem to have some opposite-sex friend, but for most, if there is a best friend, he or she is of the same sex. And there is now considerable verbal criticism of the opposite sex. Girls may remark, "Boys stink," "Too fresh," "Too rough." Boys say they don't want to be bothered with girls and accept them only as a necessary evil. Or there may be some note-writing: "I hate so and so," "So and so really likes you," or even the more direct "I love you."

Most Nine-year-olds, especially if their curiosity about reproduction has been more or less satisfied at Eight, do not show great interest in this matter. However, girls may be interested in their own role in reproduction: "Have I got a seed inside of me?" Or if they notice that their pregnant mother is getting fatter they may ask, "Will I be that fat some day too?"

Some Nines are quite self-conscious about exposing their bodies. If they are with a friend of the same sex, they may exclude a younger sibling of the opposite sex when changing clothes. Many are quite uncomfortable if by chance they should see a parent nude.

Many at Nine are quite interested in the details of their own organs and functioning and may even seek out information in an encyclopedia or reference book. Most girls now know about menstruation. Swearing, for some, has now shifted from the use of words referring to elimination to words related to sex. Rhymes that children pick up at play often have rather pointed sex implications. Children may repeat these rhymes at home to shock their mother. Neighbors may complain about the kind of language boys use.

An important aspect of sex, here as at any age, is the child's own feeling about his or her sexuality. Most parents will tell you that raising girls is a very different matter from raising boys. While in recent years some feminists have insisted that if we treated children of both sexes alike, they would be alike, observation as well as common sense tells us that that is not the case. Children of the two sexes behave differently because they *are* different, as a rule *very* different.

The basic premise of Dr. William Sheldon's constitutional psychology states that behavior is a function of structure. Thus bodies that are different in structure tend to behave differently. Boys in general (though there are exceptions) tend to be more mesomorphic (strongly and squarely built). Mesomorphs in general are vigorous, aggressive, competitive, loud, noisy, and rough. Girls in general (and again there can be many exceptions) tend to be more endomorphic. They are rounder and softer and, because of these physical endowments, tend to be quieter, more cooperative, more nurturing by nature than is the average boy.

Even in nursery school we see these differences very strongly. Girls play in the doll corner, acting out domestic routines. Boys tend to climb and tumble, to play with cars and trucks, and to build with blocks. They move about more than girls do. If encouraged to play in ways different from those suggested by their natural instincts, they soon lose interest and return to their own preferred ways of playing. These differences in preference continue well into Nine and beyond.

Nowadays most parents permit their boys to play a softer role if they so wish (we no longer tell them that "boys don't cry"). Girls have always been allowed to be "tomboys" if so inclined and today are brought up knowing that they can enter any profession (or do any kind of work) they choose. Despite these facts, in general children seem most comfortable if they are permitted to follow the paths selected by their native endowment. Parents do best when they are willing and able, as most are, to accept the old-fashioned notion that "boys will be boys" and "girls will be girls."

chapter six
GENERAL INTERESTS
AND ABILITIES

PLAY

The Nine-year-old works hard and plays hard. In fact, he is apt to overdo to the point of fatigue, even while enjoying himself. He plays football until he is exhausted, sleds till he is soaked to the hips, watches television for hours on end (if permitted), drugs himself with comic books. Whatever he enjoys he will do endlessly.

Individual differences in play interests are very strong now, so that it is harder at Nine than at some other ages to predict what will be the favorite activities. Some Nines prefer outdoor activities, while others prefer to stay indoors, reading or watching TV. Some boys spend a great deal of time involved in organized or unorganized sports. Others are definitely *not* athletically inclined. If he is engaged in any kind of sports, a Nine-year-old is more interested than earlier in improving his skills, in beating his own record, in really doing things well. Many girls, too, enjoy sports.

Some at this age enjoy hiking or bicycling; others spend a lot of time with their pets. Sex differences are pronounced. Boys like to build things with Erector sets or other constructive material, or to make models. They spend a lot of time roughhousing. Some are interested in boxing or judo. Girls in general are still strong on paper dolls, using them in dramatic play. They identify with their dolls, playing out elaborate domestic dramas or simply satisfying themselves by making or buying elaborate costumes. In fact, girls' collections may still have to do mostly with their dolls. Boys' collections are more varied.

Some of both sexes are now interested in photography and in making use of their own (or their family's) computers.

Ball play of some sort is a sure organizer of groups and for some takes precedence even over television watching. Baseball is a great favorite, but some are happier with soccer. In baseball, a highly competitive coach may give the less effective players little chance to participate. Soccer may offer more opportunity for everybody, skilled or unskilled. Some Nines also enjoy football, though their games are for the most part unorganized. Though some sort of ball play is for boys especially perhaps the favorite outdoor activity, there is a beginning interest in bowling and horseshoes, as well as a continued interest in bicycling, roller skating, ice skating, swimming, sledding, and hiking.

Indoors, Nines enjoy the more competitive table games, such as Parcheesi, Monopoly, Children's Trivia.

One of our Nine-year-old friends gave us the following listing of his favorite activities: make sand castles at the beach; go swimming; swing on swings in the playground; read books; draw pictures; ride my bike; play soccer; play baseball; play Monopoly, Parcheesi, and Chinese checkers; work on my computer; climb trees; play the piano; go fishing or catching crawdads and frogs. (Even children who do not live in the country will enjoy countrylike activities whenever the opportunity presents.)

At Christmastime, a Nine-year-old may make a long list of presents that he or she would like to receive, but most are mature enough to appreciate that probably they will not get all they ask for.

READING AND WRITING

As with other recreational activities, there are very marked individual differences in the area of reading and writing. Many Nines are omnivorous readers. Others hardly read at all, except as they are forced to in relation to school activities. Thus some children don't or can't read to any extent whatever. Others not only read avidly, but if they really like a book they may read it more than once. Enthusiastic readers often handle public library transactions on their own.

Nine-year-olds especially enjoy detective and mystery stories as well as the junior classics, such as *Tom Sawyer, Treasure Island,* and *King Arthur.* They also like to subscribe to magazines addressed to boys and girls of their age level.

Although most children of this age do enjoy the classics or modern books aimed at their special interests—the kinds of things that parents consider "good" reading—many still are great comic-book fans. While comic books do not seem to play the major role in a child's life that they used to before the advent of television, they are still extremely popular with some Nines. Children swap, borrow, hoard. But even the comic-book lovers may not buy as indiscriminately as when they were younger.

If your child seems to be going overboard on comics, you can intervene and appeal to the child's reasonableness—request that he read one or two library books now and then. However, children of this age are likely to persist in whatever they enjoy—comics, clubs, mechanical interests—with great vigor, intentness, persistence, and absorption. Nine-year-olds tend to be extremely busy with their own special interests, whatever they may be.

Most Nines no longer print but prefer to write. Their handwriting now tends to be reasonably legible and may now be put to practical use. Some children of this age keep a diary. Or they like to write lists, cataloging their collections. Both boys and girls like to order things by mail.

MUSIC, RADIO, TELEVISION, AND MOVIES

Those Nine-year-olds who have persisted in their earlier interest in music lessons may now really apply themselves. With their persistence and their interest in perfecting a skill, they often enjoy their lessons and may even practice willingly and without too much pressure, even though most do need reminding.

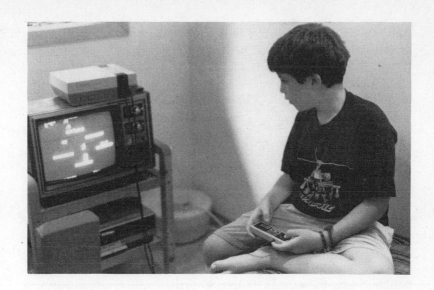

A Nine-year-old's touch is lighter than it was. This gives him better control over the sounds he produces. Many are beginning to enjoy being able to play, and fortunately in many, playing has improved to the point that the family can more or less enjoy the music.

Nearly all homes now have at least one television set, and TV is a favorite of children when playing together. Nines tend to be great TV fans. Needless to say, children of this age know the times and channels of their favorite programs. Detective programs are becoming special favorites, though most Nines still cling to a few of the children's adventure stories. They may also enjoy situation comedies aimed at children, quiz programs, and adult comedies. Some like to watch the news. However, some children, for all their enthusiasm, are not as rigid about their programs as earlier and might even miss a favorite show if something of greater interest turned up.

Many still like to listen to the radio, especially to their own transistor radio, though most greatly prefer television.

Some Nines go to the movies once or twice a month, though nowadays there seems to be less movie going than occurred a few years ago, as many are quite satisfied to stay at home and watch, on videocassette, movies their parents have rented. Nintendo is also very popular.

BODILY ACTIVITY AND EYE–HAND COORDINATION

The typical Nine-year-old is considerably more skillful than earlier in motor performance, and he likes to display his skill. His timing and coordination are now under better control. He is interested in his own strength and ability.

Boys are quick to assume an active fighting stance. They love to strike out at each other and to wrestle. They are especially interested in testing their own strength, as when lifting things.

As mentioned, both boys and girls are apt to do one thing till they are exhausted, such as riding a bicycle, running, hiking, sliding, or playing ball. Unless protected, they are very likely to overdo.

Eyes and hands are now well differentiated, and the two hands can generally be used quite independently. In most Nines handedness, in fact sidedness, has as a rule long since been well established. Fingers also show new differentiation. Nine drums them on a table, picks and fiddles and flicks or fingers the edge of the paper he is reading.

However, manual skill is quite an individual matter, and by now the child is usually said to be either good with his hands or poor with them. There is a certain fineness of discrimination, and children of this age now like to sketch, whereas at Eight their strokes tended to be bolder and larger. Most boys use tools reasonably well. They can hold and swing a hammer well, or can saw easily and accurately, using a knee to hold a board. Both boys and girls handle garden tools appropriately. And Nines like to build complex structures, as with Legos. Girls now can cut out and sew simple garments, and most are also good at knitting.

Sitting posture may now be quite awkward, in spite of the motor skill that the child shows in other respects. Both sexes may slouch in a chair or get into unusual postures. As a Nine works at a desk, his head may be quite close to his working point, since Nine is a pulling-in age. (For instance, the child may draw things smaller.) Visually the child of this age likes to hold things close. Or he may exhibit an open-eyed stare, which he maintains for some time without blinking. He may even focus without actually seeing what he appears to be looking at. (Mothers note this as their child looks right at them without, apparently, hearing what they are saying to him.)

chapter seven
THE CHILD'S MIND

Though nearly every kind of behavior described in this book is directed by the child's mind, this chapter is restricted to a few of the behaviors that are customarily considered to be examples of the child's thinking, or thought process. Thus we describe here primarily the following topics: time, space, thinking in general (including the child's ideas about death, Deity, and that old favorite, Santa Claus), different kinds of intelligence, reading, writing, and arithmetic.

Psychologist Jane Healy describes this age well when she tells us that this is a relatively calm period for many children. As academic skills from the first three grades are practiced and refined, most fourth-graders feel capable and in control. The brain strengthens its abilities for learning, as myelination of fibers speeds associations between senses and ideas. Late elementary grades are an ideal time to apply skills already learned. *Reading to learn replaces learning to read.* Math becomes useful in the shopping mall or on the computer.

Many children of this age love to soak up information and memorize facts, but they may not reflect very deeply about them. They painstakingly copy paragraphs for reports but have difficulty paraphrasing them. Lots of practice is needed—and probably some adult help with organization and understanding. Above all, older children need plenty of time for their own brands of play. They still learn best by starting with concrete experiences. The most helpful parents and the most successful teachers capture Nines' wide-ranging curiosity in active, project-oriented learning.

TIME

Nines may be said to be controlled by time rather than controlling it. Their day is filled to the brim with the many things they want to do. They are so busy that they often have difficulty in finding time to do all the extra things that are now a part of their life. Everything they do is important to them and therefore it is hard for them to give up anything. And with their characteristic persistence, they find it difficult to finish one thing in order to get on with the next. They never seem to have time enough.

However, Nine-year-olds do show signs of controlling time in that they plan their day and know what follows what. In their race with time, they may set their alarm clock for early morning, either to gain time for reading or simply to enjoy the leisure of an extra hour's sleep after they turn off the alarm.

Time conscious as the child of this age is, he very much appreciates having a wristwatch. Even with its help, as one mother put it, the child of this age seems almost to be fighting time. Certainly all too often he is pressed by it. But in all of his rush, he may be conscientious enough to phone home if, as is often the case, he finds that he is going to be late.

That time is important to the child of this age is shown by the fact that he can be challenged to show his best speed if his performance is being timed.

Nines are much interested, as they were a year earlier, in history and in ancient times, and also in the life span of various individuals. Many enjoy reading biographies of famous people written for children.

SPACE

Your typical Nine-year-old tends to be reasonably well oriented in space. He can go to familiar places, as to the dentist's or to a music lesson, on the bus by himself.

He shows an ever-expanding interest in community life, branching out from the beginning enthusiasm exhibited at Eight. Thus he shows a good interest in community problems of health, life, property, businesses, and in manufacturing and agricultural industries, matters of transportation and weather, animal and plant life in the community, and holiday and seasonal activities.

More than this, his environment expands to take in not only his community, state, country, but the whole earth and even distant parts of the universe. He likes to study cultures other than his own, is interested in China, Russia, South America. This interest, of course, is supported nowadays by the things he can see on television or—if he is a reader—that he may read in the newspapers.

And if he is a letter writer, he may enjoy corresponding with a pen pal from some distant country.

Spatially well oriented as the typical Nine-year-old may be, not all Nines are typical. As we have mentioned elsewhere, this is an age at which great individual differences make themselves evident. Thus though certainly most Nines do better with space than they did earlier, there are some boys and girls who even when they grow up will never be extremely well oriented in space. They tend to be mixed up as to directions, have trouble finding their way even in somewhat familiar surroundings, and are very poor at puzzles which require one to put together many little pieces to form a perfect cube.

Parents, teachers, or vision specialists usually notice quite quickly when children cannot see well. But when they do poorly in space, often others are not particularly aware of this fact, so that the child may stumble around for a long time before anyone notices the problem.

THINKING

For several decades the Swiss child specialist Jean Piaget has written the most about the child's mind. He has described the stages the child goes through as thinking develops. As Piaget speaks in terms of larger age ranges, rather than picturing yearly age changes as we do, he makes no distinction between the Eight- and the Nine-year-old.

According to Piaget, the Eight- to Eleven-year-old stage of thinking can be described as *concrete operational,* or a time of the beginning of abstraction. When children reach this stage they are less self-centered than earlier. They now recognize the views of others (according to Piaget). And they can correct inadequate first impressions by more or less applying the rules of logic.

Thus they know that the shape of a container does not affect the quantity it holds. Both a Nine-year-old and a Five-year-old may intuitively sense that there is more water in a tall, thin cylinder than in a flat dish in which the water rested moments earlier. But the older child subdues this intuition with a recently acquired rule that states that the amount of water in a vessel must remain the same if the only change is in the shape of the container holding it.

They also understand the idea of number. They can tell that ten marbles in a row are more than eight in a row even if the two rows are of the same length. Earlier they would have thought the numbers were the same if the rows were of equal length.

The Nine-year-old can apply simple logic to arrive at a conclusion, reasons deductively, and can now classify. Also he is able to picture a series of actions, such as going on an errand and returning. Before he reached this particular stage of thinking, he could not draw a map of where he

would go. Following a familiar route (which children can do when younger) is different from visualizing it.

Though we ourselves have never found Piaget's categories to be of great value to most parents (some teachers

claim to have found them of help), we do find that beginning in some at Seven and certainly increasing by Nine,
many children are improving in their ability to think abstractly. We ourselves have noted the emergence of independent critical thinking certainly by Nine.

Nines also are now using language to express increasingly subtle and refined emotions and shades of feeling:
disgust, self-criticism—"I *would* do that!" "Oh, I'm so
clumsy!" There is also considerable, and often fairly elaborate, criticism of their parents' actions.

It sometimes seemed that the Eight-year-old liked to talk
just for the sake of hearing himself talk. At Nine language
is used more as a tool, as to share ideas or express opinions,
and less for its own sake. There is a marked falling off in
out-of-bounds verbalization—that is, of wild exaggeration
or fantasizing or plain out-and-out tall tales, so characteristic at Eight.

We see at this age an increasingly realistic concept of the
world, less interest in fairy stories, and less belief in magic,
though some still have a strong belief in luck and may be
quite superstitious.

The Nine-year-old's concepts of such matters as death,
Deity, and Santa Claus have matured some during the past
year. Most children of this age are relatively matter-of-fact
about death. They can now look straight at it, no longer
focusing on such peripheral aspects as coffins and graves.
Now they are interested in logical or biological essentials
connected with the process of dying: You are "not living,"
"Death is when you have no pulse and no temperature and
can't breathe." An occasional Nine may say "Oh, I wish I
had never been born" or "I wish I were dead." As a rule
they do not mean these remarks literally. Death is not of
marked interest to most at this age.

Your typical Nine-year-old stays around home more than
he may have at Eight, and thus he often is not too interested in such rather remote concepts as Deity. And there
may also be a dropping off in Sunday School and church

attendance, unless the social aspect of Sunday School still holds his interest. But, as Dr. Gesell once put it, the child of this age "is taking himself in hand, almost in a spirit of rationalism."

Certainly by now he does not believe in Santa Claus. However, most would not be so ruthless as to destroy this myth for a younger sibling. Rather, the Nine-year-old smiles tolerantly and may actually enjoy a younger brother's or sister's enthusiasm. Certainly he enjoys Christmas, but Santa is not a real part of it except as something he remembers being excited about when he was younger. A typical Nine-year-old may tell you, when asked how he feels about Christmas, that it is "A time to be loving and kind."

DIFFERENT KINDS OF INTELLIGENCE

By the time your girl or boy is Nine years of age, you may have had the disconcerting experience that a child whom you considered of fully average or possibly well above average intelligence is not doing well in school. There can, of course, be many reasons for school failure or nonsuccess. One that is not often considered is that your child may not have the kind of intelligence that is taught to and respected by the school.

According to Harvard neurologist Howard Gardner, there are at least seven different kinds of intelligence, and most children demonstrate their particular strength in perhaps only one. Gardner identifies the following kinds of intelligence.

Linguistic Intelligence: Children gifted in linguistic ability think in words. If your child has this kind of intelligence, he or she may like to write, loves reading, spells easily and well, may like doing crossword puzzles or playing Scrabble.

Logical–Mathematical Intelligence: These youngsters can think conceptually. When older, they are capable of abstract and logical thinking. They may complete arithmetic problems in their heads, enjoy using computers, reason out things logically and clearly, and be good at things like the Rubik Cube.

Spatial Intelligence: These children easily locate themselves and other people in space. They are good at mazes and jigsaw puzzles, and read maps, charts, and diagrams easily. They may wish to become architects, mechanics, or engineers.

Musical Intelligence: While children with musical intelligence often play an instrument well, others may merely be specially sensitive to music and other sounds. They remember melodies, know when something is off key, and learn anything more easily if it is conveyed to them rhythmically or musically.

Bodily–Kinesthetic Intelligence: People with this sort of intelligence process knowledge through bodily sensations. They excel in competitive sports, tend to be in constant motion, love such physical activities as swimming, hiking, skateboarding.

Interpersonal Intelligence: These children understand people. They are frequently leaders among their peers. They are organizers, communicators. They have many friends and are very social and tend to be "street smart."

Intrapersonal Intelligence: Such individuals tend to shy away from group activities and may prefer to be alone with their inner feelings, thoughts, and dreams. They have strong opinions and feelings and tend to be strong-willed. They may march to the beat of a different drummer in their style of dress, behavior, and general attitudes.

Everyone has some of all seven intelligences in varying levels, but in most people some one area dominates. Unfortunately, not every child excels in the kinds of intelligence favored by our schools—linguistic and logical-mathematical.

READING

According to reading specialist Jeanne S. Chall, the child's reading abilities, like other abilities, develop through a series of patterned stages. Most Nine-year-olds have moved past her Stage 2, in which the child "unglues" himself from the print and develops fluency. In Stage 2 he does not so much gain new information as confirm what he already knows.

By Nine most children, if they are developing on schedule, reach Stage 3, the stage of reading in which the child reads to learn something new. Much earlier they were learning to read. Now they read to learn. This big step, which normally takes place around Nine years of age, when most children are in fourth grade, is difficult for some. It may be the reason that some Nines who have managed their reading earlier now start to fail.

On the other hand, some children who may have had trouble with reading earlier may now show a real spurt. Some Nines seem to do well in silent reading, though this needs to be checked by having them read aloud. Many actually prefer silent reading, but when reading for facts and information they may retain material better if they read it aloud.

A Nine-year-old tackles any word and is not too concerned if he does not know the meaning, unless it is important to the story. Most now read sentences and paragraphs with ease. Some even know how and when to skim for thought and when to read thoroughly. Also they know how and when to read for pleasure or recreation and when to read for information. Many now can use the dictionary to find simple words and in order to get definitions and pronunciations. Most can now use an index, glossary, and table of contents.

Reading errors are fewer. Almost none reverse single letters. A few, in very long or difficult words, may reverse

adjacent letters or make a slight change, as "porfisuon" for "profusion." A few sometimes reverse the order of adjacent words, repeat words, or use another word with the same meaning.

If your child is still having trouble with reading, this can be a good age to initiate a program of home training, if you keep in mind that the typical Nine-year-old is far different from what he was just a short year earlier. It is certainly a good age to set the child on the path to adequate reading behavior if there is trouble at school that has not been remedied. It is important for a mother initiating a home program to keep in mind what the child is like, to utilize aspects of his behavior that might be expected to lead to success in such a program, and to minimize or work around kinds of behavior that might jeopardize its success.

Thus while at Eight a mother might suggest home teaching as something the two will enjoy together, at Nine it is important to depersonalize the activity. Set it up not as something you are doing together, but rather as something the child himself is doing to improve his own performance.

With help from the school reading specialist if you need it, outline whatever program you select, arrange for the activities, and then stay out of things as much as you reasonably can. Set up, or let the child set up, his own goals and then let him work toward them, as independently as possible. Nine likes to do things well, he likes to succeed, he likes to outstrip his own earlier performance. But he likes to do all of this on his own.

If a mother intrudes only minimally, chances are that her help, when needed, will be accepted. If things are not too good between them, Father or some other adult may turn out, briefly, to be a more successful supervisor.

Nines are by nature excellent pupils, ready to tackle anything that lies reasonably within their powers. This is an optimal age for perfecting the proficiency of basic subjects, such as reading. The child is old enough, in most cases, to see for himself the advantage of improving his reading skills.

He now has a special interest in process and skill and is more able than earlier to analyze his movements both before and during action. He also is increasingly persistent in practicing his skills. He enjoys repetition, especially if he can see that it is paying off. That is, he is usually quite willing to stick with a task. He does not need the variety that he did when just a little younger.

Though the child of this age is not as dependent on praise as he was just earlier, a little judicious praise is appreciated. But more than praise, the Nine-year-old may enjoy the fact (should it *be* a fact) that he actually is doing better. Being as a rule less embroiled with Mother than earlier, the Nine-year-old may even be able to accept her help and to interrupt whatever else he is doing to undertake his reading exercises. However, in general it is better to have a special time set up for them, a time that he himself has helped to choose so that it will not interfere with other important activities.

Keep in mind that, as mentioned earlier, Nines are great excuse givers, great alibiers. Whatever you want them to do may "hurt" the part of the body involved. Thus their eyes tend to hurt if they have to read. A wise parent who is aware of this tendency will take rather lightly any pitiful comments that whatever is being asked of the child is hurting some part of him. Be sympathetic but firm about the fact that the planned-for exercises will proceed.

WRITING

As mentioned, most Nines no longer print, but prefer to write, and handwriting may now be put to practical use, may have become a useful tool. A boy or girl may keep a diary, or write lists, cataloging his or her collections. Both boys and girls like to order things by mail.

Penmanship, particularly in girls, is smaller, neater, and carried out with less pressure than earlier. For most, letters are relatively even and in good proportion, though boys usually still write with heavy strokes. The Nine-year-old usually maintains his writing quality long enough to complete a given task, though some Nines admit that their writing is sloppy—"My most careless thing."

ARITHMETIC

Arithmetic attracts extreme reactions. Children tend to love it or to hate it. Girls, especially, tend to hate it. (Some people maintain that it is society's expectations that cause girls to dislike arithmetic. We ourselves suspect that society's expectations have come from observing girls over the years.)

Both sexes may prefer written to oral arithmetic. In figuring out math problems, many can explain how they got their results. In addition and subtraction, most know all the simple combinations by heart. They know what combinations they have the most trouble with and like to analyze their errors with the teacher's help. Most can multiply through the nine times table, are learning to use fractions and measurements, and can on paper use two- to five-digit dividends and one-digit divisors, using the method of long division.

WHAT CAN YOU EXPECT OF A NINE-YEAR-OLD?

Parents are often interested to compare their own boy or girl with whatever "average" or norm the specialists have worked up. Here is a list of abilities developed by the National Assessment of Educational Progress, based in Denver, Colorado. You may like to check your own child's behavior against this list.

Two-thirds of a representative group of Nine-year-olds from all over this country were able to do, or know, the things listed:

Know the difference between even and odd numbers.

Can add two-digit numbers.

Can tell time.

Know that there are more stars in the universe than can be counted.

Know that clouds are a necessary condition for rain, and that snow is a likely result of cold, cloudy weather.

Know that penguins cannot fly, that fish have scales, and that rabbits eat only plants.

Are interested in people with cultural differences and are willing to help others.

Understand that unfair rules and laws can be changed.

Know that judges preside at trials.

Many know who the President is and how he is chosen.

Many are familiar with the appropriate uses of dictionaries and encyclopedias.

Many read books and stories on their own.

Many are familiar with characters from fairy tales.

Many can write without making punctuation, agreement, or word-choice errors.

Many are familiar with the basic conventions of letter writing and can write letters to friends.

Many are familiar with the names and sounds of most musical instruments.

Many can draw in perspective by having figures shown progressively higher on the picture plane.

Many can draw a running person's arms in appropriate positions.[7]

SUGGESTIONS FOR STRETCHING THE BRAINS OF NINE-YEAR-OLDS

And finally we look once more to Jane Healy for what seem to us practical suggestions for stretching the brains of Nine-year-olds:

Help them begin challenging literal fact.

"Why do we go to school only on weekdays? Why five days a week?" "Why *shouldn't* people steal?"

Let them see that there are many points of view on issues, probably *no one right answer.* Thus play games with open-ended questions: "What would you do if . . . we won the lottery? we lost all our money? you woke up one morning seven feet tall?"

Help them articulate their feelings and don't be afraid to talk about yours. ("I really felt scared when I thought Grandma was seriously ill. I bet you did too.")

Play games of strategy which require weighing alternatives, planning moves ahead, or viewing a situation from the opponent's perspective ("Stratego," "Battleship," chess, checkers, gin rummy, hearts).

Play "Twenty Questions." Show how to ask categorical questions. ("Is it an animal?" rather than "Is it a dog?")

Practice allowing the child to make some reasonable choices and to experience the natural consequences. ("If you use your allowance on the record, you won't have enough to go to the movies with the gang.") Don't weaken and bail them out of minor consequences.

If your child has trouble understanding a school assignment, look for a way to present it with pictures, timelines, maps, or objects that can be manipulated. Have fun acting out ideas or situations. Your child still learns best from concrete experience.

Get a book of simple science experiments and try some at home. Talk about possibilities of what might happen. Make guesses together, without worrying about who's right or wrong.

Have dinner together and talk with your child. Watch TV news together and talk about what happened. *Listen* to what your child is saying. Teachers are convinced that good family conversation times produce good students.

Don't stop reading aloud. Encourage memorization of
fine poetry or prose. Try round-robin family reading.
Appreciate those childlike qualities even while you help
him stretch. Remember, he still reasons differently
from you.[8]

Dr. Healy also points out special environmental factors
that can affect a child. Exposure to lead or toxins such as
formaldehyde, pesticides, or certain medications may cause
learning or behavior disorders. Parents whose work puts
them into contact with toxic substances should be aware of
the hazards of transmission to a child at home from clothing or in breast milk. Diet is important, too: A shortage of
protein may retard brain growth, and a number of food
substances are being investigated as possible contributors
to children's learning problems. In addition to keeping in-
formed about this fast-growing area of research, parents
should carefully scrutinize a child's daily environment for
any potential hazards and should consult their own doctor
if they have any questions.

chapter eight
SCHOOL

School for the Nine-year-old is something else again from what it was just a year earlier. The work demanded of the Nine-year-old fourth-grader is geometrically, not just arithmetically, more difficult than that demanded of the Eight-year-old third-grader.

Up till now it is as if the work of each succeeding grade is just a *little* more difficult than that of the preceding grade. Now comes a quantum jump. Successful fourth-grade work demands a new kind of thinking, a new kind of abstracting, a new way to use information that up till now may have been more or less memorized.

Teachers recognize this big extra requirement that fourth grade makes of most pupils, but many parents are not aware of it. Thus many are surprised when their child, successful in school up till now, suddenly runs into unexpected difficulties.

It is in part because of this extra demand of fourth grade that we warn parents of the importance of being sure that their children are properly placed, in a grade that meets their basic maturity level, right from the beginning. This is true because even though he may be overplaced, a bright child from a reasonably good home background can often slide through the first three grades.

It is often only when he enters fourth grade, with its really tough demands, that the overplaced child so clearly shows his or her immaturity. And his parents are faced with the unhappy fact that their presumably capable child is *failing* fourth grade. Then comes the question of what to do about it.

Requiring a child to repeat a grade is in most instances not too traumatic in the very early grades, but by fourth grade many parents think it is too late. It is not too late, but it would have been better to have the child repeat earlier. Better still would have been not to have started him in school, even in kindergarten, until adequate maturity or behavior tests had assured all concerned that he was fully ready.

It is hoped that your school has provided good advice about your child's proper placement right along. But if it hasn't, and you are worried now, here are some of the best clues to overplacement in fourth grade I have ever seen. If your fourth-grader is in difficulty, you may like to check these over and see if any of them apply. In using this list it is important to keep in mind that all children display some stress signs some of the time, so that if your own child expresses a few of these, it is not necessarily a sign of overplacement. Also keep in mind that some signs and signals transcend grade level and are a clue to overplacement whenever they occur.

GRADE FOUR STRESS SIGNALS THAT MAY BE SIGNS OF OVERPLACEMENT

1. Wants to play with third-graders.
2. Mixes manuscript and cursive writing.
3. Does not work well independently.
4. Sees everything that goes on in the classroom.
5. Partially completes assignments.
6. Takes in-house field trips, such as going to the lunchroom to find out what they are having for lunch.
7. Is last to be chosen for games or sports.
8. Has nervous tics: eye, throat, nose, etc.

9. Needs to be taught the same concepts over and over again, i.e. division, capitalization, punctuation, etc.
10. Worries about Grade Five.
11. Is preoccupied about "being right."
12. Constantly sneaks a peek at his or her multiplication chart.
13. Displays avoidance behavior.
14. Nightly parental assistance with homework causes family tension.
15. Constantly breaks pencil.
16. May copy another child's work when pressure is on academically.
17. Is unable to find pencil, pen, papers in his or her own desk.
18. Forgets how to set up his or her paper with name, date, subject, and margin.
19. Daydreams.
20. Needs to be re-taught concepts from the week before on Mondays and after vacations.[9]

In spite of the fact that many Nine-year-olds are faced with what for them may seem rather rigorous demands, most do enjoy school. The morning home routine of getting ready for and off to school has now largely been straightened out. It is no longer such a rush and hassle, and most girls and boys take the responsibility for getting to school themselves. However, a Nine-year-old may have trouble remembering to take his school materials with him, even though he has planned this ahead of time and has put his things in a convenient place. He may still need reminding.

The child may now report at home about school more than he used to. He especially likes to report some success or outstanding activity of his own or to tell about some special event. Because achievement is very important to the child of this age, girls and boys tend to be competitive both in work and play, afraid of failure, wanting to do their best.

In school, Nines may refer now and then to their teacher

for help, but much of the time they like to work independently. The child of this age tends to have a reasonably good critical judgment of himself. He may tell you, "Arithmetic is my best subject" or "So and so is best at art." Most have a reasonably good idea of the things they are "sure" about and of the things they do well and those they do poorly. Attention span is now longer than it was, and many can work for relatively long periods, and even be unwilling to stop unless they feel they have fully finished and have done a good job.

Though as a rule Nine-year-olds like school, nevertheless they often behave worse than when younger. This is the age when many children become dreamy and restless and "don't concentrate," especially if the work is too hard for them. However, if Nines are correctly placed in school and the work is not too hard for them, they tend to be real workers and are usually willing to put forth a great deal of effort.

With his tendency to competitiveness, the Nine-year-old likes to know what his grades are and to compare them with other children's grades. However, he is afraid of failure and tends to worry. He is also a perfectionist and makes great demands of himself. He wants to be accurate and likes to be helped to analyze his errors. He is now mature enough to understand the concept of "good" and "bad" errors (that is, errors that show that his process is right but that he has simply been a little careless, versus those that show that his process is wrong). He doesn't like things that are "too hard," such as grammar or "addressing envelopes and trying to get the address right."

Though some school systems no longer use report cards, most Nines, as just noted, do like to be graded and to compare their own grades with those of others.

All in all from the child's point of view, especially if he is properly placed, things may not be too bad. But teachers often do report that fourth grade is a difficult one to teach. This partly because children of this age are so extremely individual and so positive in their likes and dislikes. Individual differences are reported in school as in other areas of behavior, so that it is often difficult to predict just how any given fourth-grader will perform.

Also, they are not the nice, admiring little people they used to be. They want to be independent of the teacher. Even when the child needs help, the teacher's timing in giving it must be well judged. If help is offered too soon, the child is insulted; if it is offered too late, he feels neglected.

But in many ways, the teacher-child relationship at this age is much less personal than it was just earlier. The Nine-year-old tends to be more related to his subjects than to his teacher, and dislike of a teacher may now be related to a dislike of the subject that is taught. School is now more a matter of business and less one of interpersonal relation with the teacher.

Details about reading, writing, and arithmetic have been included in Chapter 7 (pages 79 through 83). We make only brief mention of them here. Thus, Nines often prefer to read silently rather than to read out loud. But they need, now and then, to be checked by means of oral reading. The child of this age is willing to tackle almost any word, even if he doesn't know its meaning. In fact, he is becoming quite an adventurous reader.

Penmanship, especially in girls, is smaller, neater, and done with less pressure. Boys may still write with heavy strokes. A Nine-year-old tends to be, and rightly so, somewhat critical of his writing. It is better than it was but still, often, not all that great.

Arithmetic is perhaps the most talked-of subject in fourth grade. It is "loved" or "hated," but despite sometimes negative emotions, most Nines do well in the subject. Children now know many number combinations by heart and know which ones give them trouble. Though the Nine-year-old likes to prove his long division, he does not yet check his own errors spontaneously. He does want to know how he made his error and enjoys analyzing his process with his teacher to find out how he made a mistake.

And just a special word about *sex differences.* A group of research analysts recently commissioned by our government to check on school behavior of a representative group of Nine-year-old girls and boys found substantial differences in the school behavior of the two sexes. They found that females outperformed males in *all* aspects of reading, writing, and literature. Females also tended to outperform males on those exercises in other subject areas that required writing skills.

Also, females tended to express more positive attitudes than males in all subject areas measuring attitudes: music, citizenship/social studies, literature, and career and occupational development. However, males clearly knew more about science and mathematics, with the exception of numbers and numeration. Literature was the chief area in which males had less *knowledge* than females, and music was the only other area in which the males' knowledge did not exceed the females'.

At any rate, in the classroom, the Nine-year-old tends to be more orderly than he used to be, and he performs his tasks with greater dispatch. An intellectual or academic problem now really challenges him. Instead of immediately looking to his teacher for support when things are difficult, he now looks within himself. The child of this age has a certain amount of self-discipline. Faced with a difficult task, if told how much he is required to do and about how long it will take, he very often proceeds on his own.

The nine-year-old puts his mind to a new task. Nines tend to work individually and are very variable from child to child, each doing whatever it is in his own way, at his own rate, and with his own degree of adequacy. Also Nines can use their spare time in school for real work, not just time-filling activity as earlier.

The nine-year-old child's typical response to school seems to confirm what we have concluded from more direct observation. It shows extreme individual differences from child to child, seemingly more than at earlier ages. It also shows, in any one child, highly variable moods with marked mood swings. There is a definite deepening of emotions, less shallowness than was observed at Eight. The child is more discriminatingly evaluative than a year earlier and highly critical of others. At Nine, many of the behavior trends of Eight, such as the child's sensitivity, become clearer. There is evidence of considerable complaining and a definite difficulty in making choices or decisions.

All in all, Nine brings a lot to school and for the most part works hard. Some teachers assure us that though fourth grade is not an entirely easy grade to teach, it is extremely interesting. At school as at home, your typical Nine-year-old is an especially endearing young person.

So far our discussion of school behavior at Nine has dealt with boys and girls who are getting on reasonably well in school and who exhibit no special problems. However, many boys and girls at every age have very special problems in learning. Here we discuss three of the more common kinds of difficulty, or categories of difficulty, that one runs into—the child who suffers from so-called dyslexia, the hyperactive boy or girl, and the one who is labeled (whether correctly or incorrectly) learning disabled. We also discuss a further kind of differentness, which may be considered a favorable kind—giftedness. And we add a word or two about an environmental situation that affects many children these days—the differentness of being a child from a single-parent family.

DYSLEXIA

We don't hear quite as much about dyslexia these days as we did during the past few decades. Children who do poorly in school nowadays are perhaps most likely to be labeled *learning disabled* (or LD). However, the term dyslexia, like many other denigrating labels, is still probably used a great deal more often than it should be.

What the term actually refers to is often merely "reading difficulty" or "reading slowly," and as Dr. Sidney Baker of our own staff has pointed out, it is no more possible to *have* reading poorly than it is to *have* running slowly. That is, it is incorrect to speak, as many do, as if dyslexia were a *disease* that people *have.*

Reading specialist Diane McGuinness, in her sensible book *When Children Don't Learn,* makes the same point. She takes exception to the general belief that having difficulty in reading involves something wrong organically, as if having dyslexia is like having leukemia. She points out that many people speak, and think, as if there is something wrong with the brains of children who do not read up to grade level or who have been labeled dyslexic.

The fact remains that boys in general learn to read a bit later than do girls. Though some feminists insist that boys are really just as good (and early) readers as girls (and girls just as good at math as boys but just *think* they are not— that is, have "math phobia"), in truth there are real and substantial differences between the sexes. At any rate, according to reliable figures over 75 percent of the children in reading-disabled groups are males.

This three-to-one ratio should be statistically impossible, says McGuinness. It occurs because we figure things wrong. Children are usually selected for remedial reading help if they are two years below the norm for their age. But in making our norms, we fail to take into account the fact that on the average boys develop reading abilities much more slowly than do girls.

Unfortunately, norms have not been provided for the two sexes separately. If girls were selected for remediation who were two years behind average reading scores for girls and boys were selected who were two years behind other boys, the sex ratio would be one to one.

Instead, remedial populations today consist of those children who are two years behind the combined average achievement test scores of both sexes. As girls are advanced compared to boys in a number of verbal skills, including reading, this procedure unduly penalizes boys.

In other words, if we figured norms separately for the two sexes, a huge percentage of boys who are now considered reading disabled would be found to be slow but within normal limits. This procedure alone would reduce vastly the number of so-called dyslexic boys. In fact, according to McGuinness, if we could establish two sets of norms, one for girls and one for boys, overnight about 10 percent of all boys—millions of them—would suddenly be normal readers for their age and sex.

So, before you accept anybody's diagnosis that your child, especially your son, is dyslexic, take a good hard look at the facts. Is this child totally unable to read, or is he merely reading below grade level? Is he perhaps, at age Seven or so, merely reversing letters in the way that a Five-and-a-half-year-old quite normally does? Does he really have a serious problem, or is he just a little bit slow in developing reading skills?

HYPERACTIVITY

The whole problem of hyperactivity, at any age, is beyond the scope of this volume. However, because many children who are having difficulties in school are diagnosed as being hyperactive, it should be mentioned briefly.

Though some speak of hyperactivity as though it were a disease, the more cautious recognize it as uncoordinated, random, unthinking, unfocused, restless, excessive movement. Hyperactivity is characterized by almost constant motions and also by excessive talking, noise-making, and generally disruptive behavior. The hyperactive child tends to be irritable, oversensitive, emotionally labile, and unpredictable in his behavior. His tolerance for frustration is low.

Not all hyperactive children are learning disabled but

many are, and certainly such children do have a hard time in school as well as at home. They give so much difficulty in school that many are treated with drugs to quiet them down. Drugs do, indeed, have a quieting effect on most, and some physicians recommend their temporary use simply to "get the child down off the wall."

However, as our colleague Dr. Ray Wunderlich points out, the all-too-customary treatment of hyperactivity with such drugs as Ritalin (methylphenidate), Mellaril (thioridazine), or Cylert (pemoline) is risky, because such drugs can impede a child's ability to learn, can cause blood disorders or eye problems, suppress appetite, or cause insomnia.

But the most important argument against the *long-term* use of medication in treating hyperactivity is that it tends to prevent a search for the true causes of this behavior. Of course, there can be many different causes, but the one doctors can often help with most is some physiological disorder, especially an allergic reaction to certain substances eaten or inhaled.

Hyperactive children often have some form of allergy; perhaps the most common kind is a neuroallergy, or "brain allergy." Every child is different, of course, but foods that are commonly implicated are sugar, cow's milk, citrus products, wheat and other gluten-bearing grains, corn, chocolate, eggs, certain nuts, fish, and berries. However, literally *any* food can cause hyperactive reactions.

Clues as to which foods do cause hyperactive symptoms can be gained from the child's diet. Usually the foods he craves, or eats most every day, or consumes in large amounts are most suspect. To discover what special foods are causing the difficulty, physicians usually recommend a medically supervised elimination diet. In choosing foods for trial elimination, one should first consider those that the child eats most frequently and in large amounts. These should be completely removed from the diet for approximately three weeks. Then they should be reintroduced into the diet, one at a time, over five-to-seven-day periods. If any of these foods is implicated as a cause of allergy or hyperactivity, it should be eliminated from the diet for at least three months.

A careful trial of this food in the diet can then be attempted. If no symptoms develop after introducing the specific food, it can then be resumed in the diet, providing the parents and physician remember that it could cause trouble if eaten in too large amounts or too frequently.

So, the well-known Dr. Ben Feingold was correct. All food additives must be considered as potential allergic or toxic troublemakers for the hyperactive child. But many physicians and parents have discovered that simply following the Feingold diet is often not enough to calm down the hyperactive boy or girl. Sugar, milk, wheat, and citrus juices are among the most common offenders, but it often takes real detective work on the part of both parents and doctor to find out what special foods are dangerous for any individual child.

Here's a letter from a mother who tells us of her gratifying success with her hyperactive and allergic son when she tried a special diet:

Dear Dr. Ames:

May I share with you the wonderful help my husband and I have been able to get for our formerly extremely hyperactive son, Raymond. Raymond, aged 9, had been on Ritalin for some time, without appreciable results. At your suggestion we arranged for visual training (in addition to being overactive he had severe visual problems). We also took him to a clinic that practices what they call orthomolecular medicine.

The results have been spectacular. This clinic changed the course of all our lives. We no longer eat sugar or refined foods of any kind. They said that Raymond's "hyperactivity" was just a reflection of his allergies and occurred at a certain period in the metabolic process.

Though his fine motor behavior is still not all that it

might be, nor is his vision by any means perfect, he most certainly is responding very positively to this homeopathic treatment which, as I understand it, is aimed at strengthening his basic constitution and improving some of his chemical imbalance.

LEARNING DISABILITIES

There are many good reasons why children have trouble learning in school. We do not by any means intend to denigrate this fact. Our feeling about the term learning disability, however, is simply that it is used too loosely and too often. It is used as if a *learning disability* were a *thing,* like mumps or measles—a thing for which there is a simple remedy, such as putting a child into an LD classroom.

Among the many reasons why children do have difficulty in learning are the following, none of which as such need be labeled learning disability.

Most often, in our experience, children have trouble in school because, though perfectly well endowed, they started the whole thing too soon and thus are overplaced.

Some children are not very bright. Though many schools tend to ignore this fact by mainstreaming, actually some children are not suited to the mainstream of education.

Often—and this is one of the more satisfactory reasons because usually something constructive can be done about it—there is something wrong with the child's biochemistry, something that can be helped by an improved diet or by protecting the child from substances to which he is allergic.

Very often, and here again something usually can be done, the child has a visual or a perceptual problem.

Or the child may have a specific reading problem, or may indeed be one who is not academically well endowed and thus characteristically does rather poorly in all school subjects. In the 1970s Samuel Kirk, a recognized specialist in this field, noted that a review of three thousand children enrolled in Child Service Demonstration Centers for Learning Disabilities in twenty-one states showed that most of the children so enrolled were general underachievers to a moderate degree in reading, spelling, and/or math. He pointed out that one can raise the question of whether such underachievement constitutes anything that can be labeled a specific learning disability.

School difficulty could result from emotional disturbance, which can often be helped by psychotherapy.

An uneven endowment can be at the root of some school difficulty. Some children, even sometimes the highly gifted, are good in some areas of performance but woefully poor in others.

In some instances the teacher's teaching style does not fit with the child's learning style. Children are sometimes taught abstractly when their way of thinking is purely concrete.

At any rate, the term learning disability is quite certainly vastly overused these days. As the late Dr. Burton Blatt commented, "America seems to have fallen in love with minimal brain dysfunction or learning disability—a popular and even more up-to-date name for what used to be called brain injury." Many of us suspect that this relatively new term, though well intentioned, may be doing more harm than good.

In those cases where its use is restricted to the perhaps 5 percent of children whose inability to perform effectively in school cannot be explained by immaturity, low intelligence, visual or hearing defects, specific reading problems, an allergic response to some substance or substances in the environment, or some other understood difficulty, the term may be correctly applied and may serve a real purpose.

But when 30 percent or even more of the children in a given school system are considered learning disabled, it seems quite obvious that the term is being used as a catchall to cover many different, and often quite unrelated, kinds of learning problem.

A more clear-cut differential diagnosis could serve two

major and useful purposes. To begin with, it could vastly reduce—more than cut in half—the number of children who are labeled LD. And among those who would still be so classified, by giving some clue as to the specific nature (so far as can be determined) of the child's problem, it can point us in the direction that must be taken to solve the problem.

THE GIFTED CHILD

Most everyone agrees that it is fine to be gifted, but many are not sure exactly how one recognizes giftedness. The most customary measure, of course, is the possession of a high intelligence. (Many put that figure at an IQ of 140 or over.) Creative ability is a second clue, even though it is often a hard thing to measure. Leadership qualities can in some be so strong that they amount to giftedness. Unusual athletic ability is another measure.

Priscilla Vail in her informative book *The World of the Gifted Child* lists further traits of gifted minds. You may like to see if you can identify any of these in your own Nine-year-old.

To begin with, for many gifted children new material seems almost more to be recognized than learned. It is as if the information, or concept, was already there and merely waiting to be quickened to life by being mentioned.

Another way in which a gifted mind reveals itself is in noticing patterns—intervals in music, shape and space in sculpture, ratio in numbers, repetitions in history.

A third characteristic of the gifted is energy, both physical energy and psychological energy.

Curiosity, though sometimes hard to live with, especially in the very young, is another characteristic of the gifted child, as are drive and concentration.

Most gifted children also seem to have unusually good memories. They also often, though certainly not always, have the gift of empathy. The genuinely sympathetic person seems to understand others intuitively.

Gifted children tend to have heightened perceptions. This trait is definitely a mixed blessing. Gifted children usually set very high standards for themselves, and their heightened perceptions can throw a painfully bright light on the discrepancy between what they would like to accomplish and what they can accomplish. (These children also tend to have very high standards for other people.)

And last, the gifted child is often characterized by divergent thinking. Not only does he not necessarily go along with the crowd, but he definitely enjoys open-ended, unanswerable questions—seeing the infinite as a treat, not a threat.

If you have identified your boy or girl as probably gifted, what next? What steps can you and the school take to see that he or she gets the best education possible?

All parents of gifted children share a common concern: What *is* the very best way to go about educating their special child? The three most common approaches are acceleration, segregation, and enrichment.

The first of these, just plain *acceleration,* is perhaps the most popular. And at the same time, it is perhaps the most damaging. No matter how gifted a child may be in certain respects, he needs to be with his agemates at least part of the time. According to Vail, "The social and emotional drawbacks to acceleration outweigh the advantages of arriving at the end of one's formal schooling one or two years ahead of schedule."[10]

Segregation, another possibility, is often provided by the very nature of the school itself, as is the case with many of the better-known secondary schools. A wise school, says Vail, "will orchestrate a good balance of rational, scientific, aesthetic and ethically moral strengths in both the student body and the faculty."[11]

And third, there is the path of *enrichment,* which can be provided in a regular school setting by means of independent projects available during school hours as part of the curriculum, or outside the school.

There are, of course, many activities that a gifted child, with a little encouragement or suggestion, can pursue on his own. These include reading, television (which is not necessarily all bad), radio, puzzles, collections.

Vail also suggests some kind of special things a child could do, such as writing a book about himself. (It does not have to be a long book.) Many would enjoy this. Or he could try a treasure hunt, an open-ended noncompetitive game that can provide hours of enjoyment. The child could choose any one of the thousands of shapes and patterns that surround us. Circles and symmetry are good examples. Then he could try to find where and how frequently his chosen pattern could be located.

Another possibility is drawing while listening to music. Another is making up picture albums.

And last, Vail suggests what she calls generative activities, those that result in a specific product. Examples are playing a musical instrument, drawing, painting or sculpting, writing, building, cooking, gardening, photography, and handicrafts.

Obviously there are many ways that the gifted child can keep himself occupied and entertained that do not involve school and that do not necessarily involve other people. The gifted child will think of many of these things himself —but sometimes a little hint from you will help.

SCHOOLS CAN HELP THE CHILD FROM A ONE-PARENT FAMILY

In the average school today, about 20 percent of the student body comes from one-parent homes. In fact, in many schools this figure is closer to 50 percent.

Commentator Vance Packard in his informative new book *Our Endangered Children* states that schools can play an important role in easing children of divorce over a crisis. "When a child's world at home is falling apart, the school can offer an island of stability and possible comfort."[12]

Here are some of the things that schools across this country have done:

The Lomita Park School in San Bruno, California, has eliminated both the Father-Son Banquet and the Mother-Daughter Tea. Instead they have an Awards Banquet for both sexes.

Some schools try to be especially aware that Mondays (after the child has spent a weekend with a noncustodial parent) can be particularly upsetting days. They try to adapt to this fact.

Teachers in some communities are being trained to watch out for special signs of trouble at home: sudden gains or losses of weight, moodiness, inability to concentrate, fatigue, attention seeking through negative behavior.

The National Association of Elementary Principals recommends that schools ease parents' burdens of child care by providing before-and-after school activities.

An obvious need in areas in which a high proportion of children come from mother-headed households is a high representation of male teachers in the elementary schools.

Schools sometimes have a hard time maintaining contact with divorced parents. As some parents feel that their marital status is their own business, some schools merely send out a standard form to all parents. It asks for names and addresses of student, mother, and father. If the card shows separate addresses for the parents, this fact is noted. The school then tries to obtain both the home and work phone numbers of both the custodial and noncustodial parent in case of an emergency.

School systems are encouraged to have books available other than the "Mommy, Daddy, Dick, and Jane" types. Some school books picture other family styles.

And some schools in which more than a third of the students come from single-parent homes offer a program on different kinds of families and on the inevitability of family change. As one girl said of such a course, "It makes you feel like you are not the only one."

Yes, as Packard puts it, it *is* a dangerous world, but all of us grown-ups, whether at home or at school, should do what we can to make life easier for children with difficult or different home situations.

chapter nine
THE NINE-YEAR-OLD PARTY

Nine is not an age for a sure-fire party. Most ten-year-olds are friendly, appreciative, and quite easily pleased with the adult's efforts to entertain them, but not so with Nines, who vary a great deal from child to child, who have very definite likes and dislikes, and who do not bother to conceal them. Some things thrill them, others bore them, and they make this quite evident. Nor do they resemble Eight-year-olds, who may themselves have a good time at a party even when their behavior is too boisterous to be satisfactory to the adults in charge.

Thus the adult who is giving a party for Nine-year-olds needs to keep in mind the outstanding characteristics of the age. If he or she does not, even quite strenuous efforts may go for nothing, since Nines are far less easily entertained, their imagination less easily caught, than when they were younger. Play activities need to be very interesting, and if possible somewhat unusual, if Nines are going to have a good time.

Knowledge of the following outstanding characteristics of the age will help considerably in the successful planning of a Nine-year-old's party.

First of all, Nines love to compete and they love to show off their (often not inconsiderable) skills. Thus competitive games involving a display of real skills are strongly recommended.

Nine-year-olds are real traders at heart. Thus a party should ideally provide both objects and opportunity for some trading to take place.

Furthermore, most Nines have an abundance of physical energy. They enjoy, and even need, plenty of games that allow them to expend this energy, and ample space (preferably outdoors) in which to expend it.

Nine-year-olds are still young enough for their behavior, especially in boys, to deteriorate quickly to sheer physical roughhousing if they are bored, overstimulated, or inadequately supervised. Careful planning, organization, timing, and supervision by strong, capable adults are therefore important.

As at other ages, an increasing number of parents today choose to give the party at Burger King, McDonald's, or some other of the many restaurants that specialize in children's parties. This is easier on the parent, if not on the pocketbook.

Or, as earlier, some families prefer to start the party with a visit to a bowling alley, miniature golf course, or whatever similar activity the community provides. This also at least cuts into the time when guests will need to be entertained by parents of the host or hostess.

KEYS TO SUCCESS

The key to success here, even more than at other ages, is that there should be very careful preplanning. Such planning avoids two opposite dangers. Nines easily either get out of hand or get extremely bored. Either of these can, obviously, ruin a party. Parties for Nines need to use up the children's tremendous energy and also offer a constant challenge. The most effective activity is a series or relay games in which either individuals, or two teams, compete. Some central theme, such as a Wild West or pirate theme or maybe a baseball theme, both stimulates the children's imaginations and helps to organize and unify the party.

Number of Guests: Because of the competitive team activities that go over so well, it is important to have an even number of children. Nine guests plus host or hostess is a good number. Most children prefer a one-sex party.

Number of Adults: Mother and one or two adult helpers (including Father if available) and possibly an older sibling should supervise. Adults need to be firm and confident and to give directions about situations clearly and definitely.

SCHEDULE

A party for Nine-year-olds can be expected to last as long as three hours. Thus a party might be held from noon to 3

P.M., with relatively hearty food provided at the end of the first hour, and the ice cream and birthday cake only during the last half hour.

Assuming that the party is to be given at home with no

trip to a bowling alley or other center of entertainment, the schedule could be somewhat as follows:*

12:00–12:10 Children have been invited to wear clothing appropriate to the theme of the party. No costumes should be bought—rather, children are to wear jeans and sweaters or jackets. A sign at the entrance of the yard can indicate that this is the D.Y. (or whatever the child's initials are) Ranch. Guests are at once "branded" with the ranch brand (adhesive tape stuck onto their jeans).

12:10–12:20 Treasure hunt, called "The Roundup." Appropriate "treasures"—such as sheriff's badge, horseshoe nail, arrow, bandana, saddle blanket, rope, small figure of a cow, wagon wheel—are hidden about the yard.

12:20–12:50 A series of competitive games involving individual skills. Good games include the following: Calf Roping, which consists of riding a three-foot stick home and at the same time kicking a ball toward (and eventually into) a paper bag anchored at the end of a twenty-foot path. Each contestant is timed. Filling the Trough is played by having the contestants run carrying a narrow-neck bottle filled with water, which they empty into a saucepan. This, too, is timed.

12:50–1:20 Casual lunch consists of sandwiches in paper bags, which can be taken into the house and eaten. Cocoa could be served from a large coffeepot. Cowboy records or someone playing a guitar furnishes a musical background. Guests may at first listen and then later join in singing.

1:20–1:40 Quiet activities indoors and opening of presents. A sample game is Horse and Rider in which children, while blindfolded, draw a horse on paper. They take

---

* We are describing a Wild West party. If you choose a different theme, make up your own schedule and details along the lines indicated. If all of this seems like too much work, you may indeed prefer to stage the party at a local fast-food restaurant.

their hands off the paper and then, still blindfolded, draw a rider.

1:40–2:25 Team relay games outdoors. Each relay should be given a different cowboy-type name. In Wild Horse Race, for instance, each person rides a stick horse to a given goal and back again to the team. In Beware of Rattlesnakes, children run, or again ride a stick horse, between balloons that are scattered between two parallel strings. The purpose is to jump over the balloons without breaking them. Bronco Riders' Relay is a variety of leapfrog. One child rushes ahead and crouches on the ground and another runs and jumps over her. Then she crouches and the next girl jumps over her, till the goal is reached.

2:25–2:35 Guests may wish to rest briefly. In fact, they may collapse, worn out by team games.

2:35–3:00 Guests return indoors for the awarding of prizes for both individual and for team games, for the giving of favors, and for eating birthday cake and ice cream.

HINTS AND WARNINGS

The Wild West party is one of the harder parties to give because it requires so much planning and so much supervision. There is always the danger that guests may wrestle, read comic books, or simply sit around being bored. But it can, if successful, be one of the most rewarding, because children of this age enjoy a good party so much and express their enjoyment so openly and freely.

As good weather is essential, the party may need to be postponed until a clear day. Fortunately, most Nines can accept this delay and disappointment.

As competition and the wish to win are strong at this age, the makeup of the relay teams should be changed frequently. Otherwise a poor contestant might obstruct the progress of one team.

This is a great age for trading. Guests may want to trade

not only prizes and favors but even their sandwiches. Thus there should be a variety of sandwiches available.

Prizes are important at this age, as at any age. However, since there is so much pleasure in achieving or in winning, the actual prize-giving can be postponed until the end of the party, and all prizes given at once.

Good prizes (prizes may be selected by the winners, in turn, from a tray) include: Scotch tape, little notebooks, combs, toy white mice, rub-on transfers or stickers, small packs of cards, and gilt-covered chocolate coins. Prize winners may be determined as follows: Each winner of an individual competition, and each member of any winning team, receives a stamp mark on the back of her hand. The total number of marks received can determine first, second, third, and booby prize winners.

IF THE PARTY IS GIVEN FOR BOYS INSTEAD OF GIRLS

Roughly the same plan may be followed if the party is given for boys instead of for girls. However, boys are more likely to get into wrestling or roughhousing in a tightly organized party. Thus more widespread outdoor activity will need to be provided. The treasure hunt could be expanded: They might, for instance, dig for treasure.

Boys, particularly, like to show off any skills they may have in competition. Thus some activities such as those appropriate to an Olympic Games theme could be introduced into the program. Also, boys of this age like to make things from models. Guests could make models of objects that would fit into the theme of the party.

chapter ten

STORIES FROM REAL LIFE

BILLY PREFERS HIS FRIENDS TO HIS MOTHER

Dear Dr. Ames:

Billy is my first and only child, and perhaps that is why his present attitude is so hard for me to take. My son has always been quite a mother's boy. And especially in the last year or two we have done everything together.

Now all of a sudden he sort of brushes me off. For instance, it comes time to go to the movies and I get ready to go and he kind of mutters that he is going with one of his friends. Also, we used to watch so many television programs together. Now it seems as if one of his friends is always in, and even if I stay and watch too he pretty much ignores me.

I'll admit it may seem a little babyish of me to mind. I know that children eventually do grow away from their parents. But so soon?

Yes, so soon! Billy's behavior doesn't mean that he no longer values you as a mother. But it is clear that he, like many other Nine-year-olds, no longer thinks of you as a playmate or as his primary friend.

This is one of the hardest lessons that mothers have to learn. The Eight-year-old child is, very often, "all mixed up with" his mother. He wants her attention and he loves her company. She is often his favored and chosen companion for the movies, for playing games, just for company. Some mothers do find this a little exhausting, but it is at least flattering that your child likes you and appreciates your company.

So it does come as a shock when all of a sudden you are no longer invited to play a starring role in his or her life. Be assured, all is not lost. There will still be plenty of things that you and Billy, or your whole family, can do together, though admittedly at this age many children enjoy family outings more if a same-age friend is included.

At any rate, try to think of Billy's change in attitude as a normal growing up and branching out, and not as a rejection of you.

Chances are, if you stop to think of it, it isn't just you that Billy seems to be ignoring. Probably it is other grown-ups as well. We once knew a little boy whose mother admonished him, "Come in and say 'hello' to your Aunt Mary. She's leaving for Florida tomorrow."

"Aw, what do I care?" replied the boy. "Anyway, the fellers are waiting for me."

Not very polite, it's true, but accurately expressing his typical Nine-year-old lack of interest in relatives or other adults. A mother, father, or even teacher can give a whole set of important directions to a child of this age, looking right at him as they do so. And he, looking right through them, may ask when they have finished, "What did you say?"

"He refused to go to his own cousin's wedding" was the reason one mother gave for referring her Nine-year-old son to our institute for help. She felt that such a lack of family feeling must be a sign that something was seriously wrong with her boy.

So, Mom, you are by no means alone.

LITTLE GIRL PUTS WORST FOOT FORWARD
IN PRESENCE OF HER FATHER

Dear Dr. Ames:

We have a Nine-and-one-half-year-old daughter who is the eldest of three. She is a very nervous, excitable child, always in a hurry, and somewhat of a perfectionist. Her father is a very unaffectionate, undemonstrative person. He doesn't believe in kissing or caressing the children. This daughter, Maxine, is very fond of her father, but she gets awfully nervous as soon as he steps into the house.

She jumps around and acts childish in front of him. He scolds her and tells her to settle down, a phrase he uses too often. She gets in a giggling mood whenever he does or says anything the least bit comical.

Another big problem presents itself at the supper table. She eats too fast and forgets her table manners. Her father gets provoked with her and runs her down. She is of normal weight and size and in good health, but her nerves are bad.

Don't you agree that her actions are perfectly normal for her age? I am quite confident she will develop nicely. My husband doesn't believe people have emotional problems caused by physical factors they cannot control. He couldn't understand my moodiness during pregnancy. Otherwise he is a good father and doesn't spank the children, which I wish he would occasionally do. His entire side of the family believes in suppressing their emotions.

Perhaps I can get my husband to read your answer and if not, I'll read it to him. Would you suggest getting Maxine a mild sedative? My doctor is letting me decide.

It's too bad that Maxine doesn't have an easier relationship with her father. Undoubtedly she is at her worst in the family group. Would your husband ever take her out alone with him? If such an excursion were, her manners might be excellent.

Table manner are often overemphasized. Perhaps you might try to restrict your husband's criticisms to two or three days a week—times when Maxine knows it's Daddy's day to criticize. (Of course, your husband might call this idea ridiculous and might flatly refuse to go along with it. But if he did agree, she might very well shine on those days, pulling her behavior up to please him.)

Is there any way you can seat her so that your husband doesn't have quite such a front-row seat for her performance at the table? Does she sit next to you?

Do you help her to do things and plan things for her father? Such planning often helps a father to a smoother, more natural relationship with a child like this. A sedative does not seem especially indicated, though sometimes we do find that certain foods to which a child may be allergic do cause some children to be overactive. At any rate, it's not likely that your husband is going to change, so your best bet is to do what you can to help Maxine behave more calmly.

TATTLING BEHAVIOR SHOULD GO UNREWARDED

Dear Dr. Ames:

I am forty, mother of four. My problem is my daughter, Patty, aged nine. Her weakness is she's always going to tell her father on me. She also tattles about her brothers and to the neighbors about their children. She is a real tattletale. She seems to enjoy seeing others punished.

I myself am a weak personality. Do you think and believe that there are strong, self-confident people and others like myself who are naturally weak? (I prefer to think of myself as casual-living rather than lazy.)

I'm afraid Patty won't be liked at school if she continues to tattle. Do you think I should get her to be more active in town activities? Would that help?

Your first problem first. When Patty threatens to tell her father on you, deal with it as you would with any black-mail. Just tell her, "Go ahead." If the relationship between you and your husband is in any way friendly, no one of your children should have the power to make real trouble between you. We assume that the things you are doing are not all that bad.

Telling on you seems to be just one part of Patty's whole problem. Of course you have to ask, why does a child need the satisfaction of tattling and of seeing others get punished? You might try to find ways to give her more positive satisfaction so that she might not need to tattle.

At any rate, it is important for you, easygoing or not, to see that her tattling is not rewarded. Most mothers manage to cut it off by simply saying "I'm not interested. Don't tell me." If you can't do that, you have a second line of defense. Unless you absolutely have to, don't punish the child who has been tattled on.

To a large extent, this will spoil Patty's fun. Even a Nine-year-old can learn fairly quickly that a certain way of behaving is not going to be rewarded. If you don't listen to her in the first place, and in most instances don't punish the others after she has tattled, and just tell her "Go ahead" when she says she's going to tell her father on you, this whole way of behaving is not going to be very satisfactory to her for long.

Yes, we do believe that there are strong, confident, independent people and others who are gentler, more easygoing, less self-reliant. Probably anybody can improve herself (or himself) a little. But it is most difficult to change your basic personality.

Do indeed try to involve Patty in a few more of the town activities. Many of these children who are quite unpleasant at home behave remarkably well outside the home and away from their family. Many Nine-year-olds like to have activities planned for every afternoon. And keep in mind that time is on your side. Patty may become a much nicer person when she turns Ten.

SHOULD PARENTS DISAGREE ABOUT DISCIPLINE IN FRONT OF THE CHILD?

Dear Dr. Ames:

Please! Print your advice on the harmful effects a child receives when two parents disagree in front of the child, where one parent has administered punishment and the other criticizes his spouse because the punishment was unjust.

Yesterday I insisted that my Nine-year-old daughter finish her breakfast or she would be late for school. She chose not to eat it, sat at the table crying, and her father quarreled with me that this was no way to treat a child. The outcome—Mother gave her a note excusing her lateness and Father drove her to school. (I do admit that I shouldn't have forced her to finish her breakfast, since she is usually a fine eater.)

However, am I not correct that at all times, even though a parent has used bad judgment in discipline, both parents must *always* refrain from criticizing each other in front of the child? My husband will not accept the long-lasting harm this can do in molding a child's character.

We do agree with you, in general. Like most child specialists, we have frequently stressed the fact that in those cases where parents disagree as to matters of discipline, it is best for them not to express this disagreement in front of the child.

However, we get the impression that you are planning to tell your husband what we have said and that you somehow expect that he will accede to the rightness of our statement. Actually, it seems most unlikely that a statement from us or from any other outsider will change his behavior in the least.

It seems to us that you are going to have to solve this problem by use of ingenuity rather than by a head-on attack. The instance you described is a good example of where to begin. You yourself admit that you perhaps did wrong to insist that your daughter finish her breakfast or be late for school. More and more, if you really put your mind to it, you will find that you are able to avoid bringing about disciplinary crises while your husband is at home.

As a rule, when there is disagreement, it is the mother who has to give in. She can use her type of discipline in the daytime, but when Father is at home he will usually use his. This may seem wrong to feminists, but it is life. Fortunately, most children learn very easily what they can expect from different people. Results are not always ideal, but things do work out.

Thus we believe that you are quite right that it is best for parents to agree. But we think that you exaggerate when you phrase it that "both parents must *always* refrain from criticizing the other in front of the child." Disagreeing isn't a good thing to do—but if other conditions in the home are good, and if the parents' relationship to each other is basically a good one, the result of disagreement is not always deadly.

NINE-YEAR-OLD BOY EXPECTS MORE ATTENTION AND PRIVILEGES THAN YOUNGER SIBLINGS

Dear Dr. Ames:
Could you perhaps suggest some ways for me to help my son who is not, I fear, a very happy child. Tommy is now Nine and a half. Increasingly, for two years—I feel that if a "phase" lasts more than a year it is more than a "phase"—he has apparently had a fear that the other children in the family, except the very youngest, will get more of something than he, or get away with something he can't. The house is usually in an unhappy uproar when he is at home.

Much as I love him, I must admit that the peace and quiet are wonderful when he spends the night with one of his friends. I can find no real basis for this feeling of his—being the oldest he has more allowance, more privileges, more freedom, than the other children. These he accepts as his natural right, but that more work and responsibility go hand in hand with more freedom he either cannot or will not see.

In the morning Tommy is usually running around screaming in a most vindictive voice that one or another of the children has not made his bed or hung up his pajamas—and Tommy is usually in his underwear, his pajamas on the living-room floor, and his bed a shambles.

If another child's godmother remembers her godson's birthday and Tommy's forgets his, he is moody for weeks. If the shoe is on the other foot, he not only thinks it natural and right, but taunts the other children with it until they cry.

Well, there it is. What on earth can I do about it? Is this behavior at all "normal" for his age?

Your son sounds like the kind of child who would greatly profit by going away to school. But you have to be very careful in your selection of the school. You want one that would give him the feeling of home, where he could have someone help him over his hurdles. He obviously needs to learn to share, to learn that fairness does not mean complete equality.

Does Tommy belong to Cub Scouts? This type of group activity is often very helpful for a boy like this, who often responds better to a Scout leader than to a parent. As your son is Nine years old, you could try talking things over with him. Tell him that you realize his difficulty and that having to share and not always have just the same as the others is hard for him.

However, it may take a lot more than belonging to

Scouts, or talking things over with you, to help your son to a happier approach to life. In his case we would definitely recommend that you seek the help of a child specialist—not by letter but in person. A number of sessions with a qualified child specialist could do wonders for your son and would be well worth any money spent.

CHESTER'S BEHAVIOR IS INDEED YOUNG FOR ONE OF HIS AGE

Dear Dr. Ames:

My problem has my husband and me, and the school, all at our wits' end. Our son Chester, Nine years old this past November and in fourth grade, still is not toilet-trained. He has perhaps not daily but very frequent toilet accidents either at school or at home. Actually there are more days when he has accidents than when he performs as he should. I am trying to train him to an after-supper functioning, but so far without too much success.

Our doctor says there is nothing physically wrong with Chester to account for these lapses. Needless to say, he is not doing well in school, but the teacher thinks this is largely because of his anxiety about his embarrassing toilet accidents. We've had him to a psychiatrist for the past six months now, but things have not improved. What can we do now?

The first thing you can do is to seriously consider grade placement. By age alone, Chester is young for fourth grade. Correct school placement by no means solves all problems, but it can help. Your son is clearly immature for his age, as his behavior shows. Most boys are well trained for bowel function by three years of age if not sooner. Some few still do have trouble in this department as late as six years of age, and this difficulty is expressed at school as well as at home. But Nine years of age is way beyond any expected outside limit.

So, because neither pediatrician nor psychiatrist can find

any "reason" for this behavior or can help you to improve Chester's behavior, you're going to have to treat him like a much younger child. You are fortunate that the school will accept him, messy as he seems to be. So he can still attend school.

But you will need to give him the kind of supervision that a very young child needs. That is, his time of functioning will still have to be more up to you than up to him. As you are going to try to set the time, for heaven's sake, have it early in the day. If you wait till after supper, this gives him all day long to have his accidents.

Though your school keeps children for lunch, you might do well, as you say you live fairly nearby and do have a car, to call for him at noon and take him home for lunch. If he hasn't had a bowel movement in the morning, perhaps he could at noon. Whether he does or not, you will presumably drive him back to school and then perhaps pick him up again after school. And if he has not functioned earlier, insist, as much as you can, that he go to the bathroom before he goes out to play.

Just what is behind this discouraging behavior we can't say. Is it sheer immaturity? Is it some need to control you, and his surroundings, by behaving in this unattractive way? Often such problems are finally solved without anyone ever being absolutely sure just why they came about in the first place. You can only try, day by day and hour to hour, to see if you can't help your son behave like the big boy he is.

However, one thing you could do is to check with a good pediatric allergist. We have known of rare cases where removal of some special offending food from the diet has helped a child control even rather severe toileting problems.

NINE-YEAR-OLD'S INTEREST IN
SEX WORRIES MOTHER

Dear Dr. Ames:

I have received helpful advice about my nine-year-old son, David, from you on several occasions during the last two years. Our present problem is sex again. He does not attempt to approach his dad about this but always me, and I have always answered him truthfully.

Now, how do you suggest I handle his newest development of dirty words, dirty pictures, dirty jokes? I have never raved and ranted over "bad" words, and he has always felt very superior over having such an understanding mother. I want to retain our healthy relationship, yet just how do I react to these horrid cartoons he brings home, for instance? Am I bending over backward too far by not forbidding them in the house but only restricting them to his own desk, and treating them with mild disdain and distaste? He knows they are "not nice" and he knows that I "understand how children are interested in all these new ideas, and like to say and talk about all these things." He brings all this stuff home to me!

It sounds as if David is one of those fortunate boys who, with a little good handling, slips quickly through the various problems with which growth faces him. This is often one of the ways in which the child specialist can tell whether it is going to be necessary to worry about (or to take drastic steps about) some problem of child behavior. The child who gets stuck in bad behaviors is the one we worry about.

You and David seem to have an unusually good relationship, and you especially seem to be doing a good job in giving him information about the various aspects of sex. Actually it is more common than many people think that the mother gives the growing boy this information rather than, as tradition dictates, the father.

Now as to this new development, it is coming in a little early. Some of the most prevalent humor at Nine and Ten has mostly to do with elimination. Usually sex joking (dirty jokes) and use of sex words comes in a little later.

As this does seem to be a natural and almost inevitable stage of coming into knowledge about sexual matters, it is extremely important that parents do not either rave and rant about it or blame the "bad children" who are teaching your good child these bad things. Your own attitude is excellent. We think you are correct not to completely forbid this kind of talk and literature. You are also, in our opinion, correct to let him see that you do not care for this kind of thing but that you can understand that children are interested in these new ideas. We think that it is a good thing at this age and stage if a child does share these things with his mother, even though his mother, naturally, doesn't enjoy this sharing very much.

It is not always the content of a confidence that matters, as much as the fact that the child wants to share his confidences with his mother. David has come to this early, but it is a perfectly natural step on the path of development; and we think that you are handling the situation with considerable skill.

BOY EXPERIENCES DIFFICULTY IN GETTING TO SLEEP AT NIGHT

Dear Dr. Ames:

I have a problem that needs some expert advice. My son, who is just Nine years old, has gotten to a point where he cannot seem to go to sleep at night. This started about two months ago. Each night when he got into bed he would develop a pain in his stomach. He would cry and fuss and get everyone upset.

I thought the pain was mostly imaginary, but took him

to our doctor to check. The doctor said there was a slight disturbance and prescribed medicine for it. Since that time Alex has developed what seems to be a habit of not going to sleep until ten, eleven, or even later every night. I get so upset and angry with him. I know I shouldn't, but my patience has really worn thin. And I also worry because he still sometimes complains about his stomach.

Each night there is something that he fusses about for hours. If my daughter, who is Thirteen, sleeps in his room, he is not too bad. But she wants to stay up later than he does and to sleep in her own room.

I have tried punishing him, taking away privileges, etc., and he promises time and time again he will be a good boy at night. But when bedtime comes he is off again. It just seems as if he can't stop fussing and go to sleep.

As I write this it doesn't seem too serious a thing, but honestly I just dread his bedtime each night because I know what is coming. No one can relax until he goes to sleep. I worry because I feel he doesn't get enough sleep, and I wonder if I am to blame that a little boy that age worries the way he does. If he gets a pain in his side he imagines it's a heart attack. And he dreams a lot.

Stomach pains and other pains are, of course, quite customary in Nine-year-olds, often without any apparent physical cause. Also, many children of this age do have trouble in getting to sleep. Not getting to sleep easily in itself is not necessarily harmful. But if your son fusses and makes trouble for the family, and is himself worried, that, of course, is a nuisance.

The fact that he is good if his sister sleeps in the room with him suggests that he may be one of those many boys who needs some kind of company. Sometimes a dog of their own, which can sleep in the room with them, solves the problem. Would you consider trying this?

As to his pains and aches, it was wise for you to check

with your doctor. However, you did this, so you can be reasonably certain that there is no clear physical problem. And it is true that at this age this kind of complaint often does occur without good physical cause.

Do you chat with your son after he's in bed to let him tell you about his day? Maybe more things are on his mind than you realize. It is astonishing how well a child relaxes when he can communicate freely. Maybe you can figure out together other ways to help him relax. Would soft music on the radio help?

However, if the stomach pains and the sleep difficulty persist, you may choose to do what so many other parents have done—consult with a child therapist. We remember one patient of ours, like your own a Nine-year-old boy, whose stomach pains were so severe that the doctor actually operated. Nothing was found, so his parents brought him to us. If you will believe it—his stomach difficulty seemed to have started when the family killed and ate one of their ducks. It turned out that in his mind that was his own pet duck. . . . Once this was discovered, and recognized, things cleared up in fairly short order. This, of course, seems like a rather extreme case. But children are strange little creatures, and often we have little idea of what goes on in their minds or their bodies.

TICLIKE BEHAVIOR MAY BE THE
RESULT OF FAULTY VISION

Dear Dr. Ames:

My Nine-and-a-half-year-old daughter, Dorothy, has trouble with total head and stomach ticing. For a while she stopped jerking her head so much. But even when she did stop, I felt it was just below the surface. I could see her neck muscles tense, and I'd know we were in for another session.

I had her to our family doctor, who tried tranquilizers. He tended to shrug off her trouble and thought it would solve itself. He did suggest separating her from her sister, Jane, who is Eleven and shared the same bed. He felt she was not getting the proper rest.

After two weeks I called him again to report that she had not improved. He then referred me to a psychiatrist. We talked to the psychiatrist but he said it might take twelve visits to be able to help her and we are not in a position to afford this.

Dorothy dreaded returning to school—does not get on with her teacher. She is a compulsive talker in school. My husband feels she just has not found her place. She is the middle child. She seems to do everything wrong. Lately if anything disturbs her she crawls under the bed or covers, and rocks. She has always been a bed-rocker. She demands so much attention that we push the other two aside, and still she is jealous of them.

What do you suggest—short of disposing of the other two so she won't be a middle child?

We're afraid you can't blame all of Dorothy's problems on the fact that she is a middle child. Middleness may complicate matters, but it doesn't cause her difficulties. There are much more basic problems to consider.

For instance, is she overplaced in school? She may be, since you say her birthday is in August, she is small, and the fourth-grade work seems to have been too much for her. Often children do quite well up to fourth grade even when they are overplaced, but the real strain begins then. Overplacement could be at least part of the reason for her poor behavior in school and her extra ticing as well.

And though this may seem rather farfetched, another thing to consider is whether there may be something wrong with her vision. Whenever we have a child who rocks, or who rocked when younger, we want to know more about how his or her eyes work and whether the two eyes work well together. To find out about this you would, of course, need to consult a visual specialist, one who specializes in what we call developmental optometry.

Most professionals do not attack a tic directly. Few direct approaches have lasting, if any, effect. Rather we try to find out, if we can, what is bothering the child and then try to make life in general smoother and easier for her. We suspect that for some time to come your daughter may respond with ticing whenever the going gets too rough for her.

THIS GIRL NEEDS VERY SPECIAL HELP

Dear Dr. Ames:

My Nine-year-old daughter, Andrea, is very bright and gets good marks in school and gets along well with her friends. During the past year, however, she has developed what seems to us like an excessive interest in cleanliness. Every time she comes in she washes her hands. She doesn't want her towels in the bathroom near the rest of the family's. Or her clothes near the other children's.

She doesn't want to touch light switches or doorknobs because other people have touched them. All of this worries me. Would sending her to camp this summer be any help?

Many seemingly eccentric behaviors that some children exhibit at certain ages (for instance, eye blinking or other ticlike behavior) seem to be characteristic of these ages and are not necessarily a sign that anything is seriously wrong with the child in question.

Even certain small compulsions—having to touch things several times in succession, having to practice certain minor rituals—are not necessarily too adverse. But your daughter's behavior seems excessive and probably outside of normal limits. Such behavior is usually thought of as an outward sign of something wrong inside. We would advise you to check with a local child specialist. If your doctor can't suggest one, call your local Family Service Agency or mental health clinic and ask them to recommend somebody.

We have known of cases where sending a child away to boarding school has been able to put an end to the kind of behaviors you describe. We once knew a girl who, like your daughter, did not want her clothes to touch anybody else's. Did not even want her clothes hung beside those of others on the clothesline. And when her brother sat on her bed, she insisted on having a new mattress. Strange to say, after a year at boarding school she had forgotten all of these concerns.

Summer camp alone would probably not do too much good except that it would get her away from the rest of the family. How she would feel about having her things near those of her campmates we don't know.

IS THIS NINE-YEAR OLD HYPERACTIVE?

Dear Dr. Ames:
I have one of the most active Nine-year-olds you could ever imagine. It seems to me as if he is never still and he has so much energy. This, of course, has its good side. He accomplishes a lot and is very good at sports.

His school, however, looks rather askance at the fact that he finds it hard to sit still, and even I, his mother, do find his constant moving around very trying. The school has gone so far as to use the term hyperactivity in relation to Josh. How can I tell if my son really *is* hyperactive, or just a bit more active than average?

The label hyperactive, like so many other labels pinned on children, does tend to be overused. Your own pediatrician is probably your best authority, since he knows your son. I suggest that you check with him.

However, just as a start you might like to try a behavior inventory for checking hyperactivity provided by Dr. William Crook, a Tennessee pediatrician, and Laura J. Stevens, in a very useful book *Solving the Puzzle of Your Hard-to-Raise Child.* Dr. Crook suggests that you consider the following thirty-five items, giving a score of 0 if the item never applies to your child. Give a score of 1 if it occasionally applies, a score of 2 if it often applies, and a score of 3 if it usually applies. Here are the items:

Overactive	Temper tantrums
Doesn't finish projects	Doesn't listen to whole
Fidgets	story
Can't sit still at meals	Defiant
Doesn't stay with games	Irritable
Wears out toys and	Hard to please
furniture	Cries
Talks too much	Is reckless
Talks too loud	Unpopular with peers
Doesn't follow directions	Impatient
Clumsy	Lies
Fights with other	Accident prone
children	Wets in daytime
Unpredictable	Wets bed at night
Interrupts	Destructive
Teases	Can't read well
Doesn't respond to	Can't write well
discipline	Performs poorly in other
Gets into things	schoolwork
Speech problems	Hard to get to bed[13]

No child, even the very best adjusted, would be expected to get a score of zero, and none of these behaviors alone is too unusual. Anyway, add up your scores. Obviously, the lower the child's score, the better things are. However, if your child's score is between 15 and 30, you might consider that he or she may be mildly hyperactive. If the score is between 30 and 45, you might consider him to be moderately hyperactive. And if the total score is over 45, it seems safe to say that he probably *is* hyperactive.

SOME CHILDREN SEEM TO BE
NATURAL-BORN DAWDLERS

Dear Dr. Ames:

We have three lovely children—a boy who will be Nine this week, a daughter Four and one-half, and our delightful baby son, seven months.

Our oldest boy and his dad are in the Little League together, and hunt and fish. Dad is son's Sunday School teacher. Big brother and sister wait on the baby and maintain there never was a funnier, cuter baby—and baby rewards us with chuckles and dimpled smiles and I suppose will eventually be just terribly spoiled.

My problem, which is truly a minor one though very exasperating, is with soon-to-be-Nine and his getting dressed in the morning, or in fact getting ready for anything. Have you any tricks up your sleeve to speed up this annoying before-school problem?

He rises early, six-thirty, and reads and plays, warms up baby's bottle. Then the rest of the family gets up and from then till he leaves at eight it's a constant "Get dressed now," "Hurry and dress," and so on.

I told him this morning I thought I would go jump in the river and when they asked "Why did she do that?" the answer would be "Oh, her son would never get dressed in the mornings and she was tired of it all."

Of course he laughed uproariously. He has always been easy to handle, and I know this procrastinating stage will no doubt pass. But there must be some fairly painless way to handle it while we are in the midst of it, since I must confess, I am tired and so is Daddy. All through breakfast there is the constant reminding of son, "You now have exactly ten minutes left to dress and eat before schooltime."

Your boy's problem is probably not just a passing phase but is, we suspect, deeply rooted in his personality. Ordinarily this dawdling behavior clears up by Eight, because children are so eager to get off to school that there tends to be no further problem.

Boys like your son seem to be natural dawdlers. They become insensitive to any instruction from the home. The only thing that finally blasts them into improved behavior is to have to face failure. That is, it sometimes works best for you to stop being responsible and let them see what happens when things are just left up to them.

How does your boy get to school? If he doesn't catch the transportation provided for him, perhaps you could let him figure out for himself how to get to school. That is, of course, rather a painful way to go about things. But a little experience of failure—and hands off from you—may be what you will have to try. Just let him realize that he is the one who has to get to school—not you.

On the other hand—a quite different approach—instead of nagging at him and reminding him, since he has such a good relationship with his father, Father could make a rule that your son get dressed just as soon as he gets up—before warming the baby's bottle, before doing any reading or playing, before eating breakfast, he must get dressed. That should be the very first thing he does. Modern parents, with their more permissive ways, sometimes forget that our own parents just made the rules and we pretty much obeyed them. Or else.

HOW TO DEAL WITH IMPATIENT BOY

Dear Dr. Ames:
I have a problem with my older son, Terry, who was Nine last January. How can I teach him patience and slow him down? He is naturally the wiry, nervous, extreme active type. My other boy, Tim, is Seven and (as so often happens) exactly the opposite. Terry is so impatient

that it is difficult for him to do handicrafts at Cub Scout meetings (although he usually does have something to show for his efforts). He is not abnormal in his work, but just terribly impatient and seldom finishes his projects at home.

The other boy can make most anything and often helps Terry with his work. I know Terry takes after me for I was always starting and dropping projects when I was a little girl. Mother just couldn't seem to get me going. So what I want to know is how do I strike the spark in Terry.

Since I understand his problem and know just how he feels, I can't scold or push him, for I don't want to antagonize him. But at the same time I wish I could train him in some way so that he will accomplish things as Tim and his daddy do. Both boys are doing well in school. Terry's only big trouble seems to be that he is in such a rush. As you can readily see, my cry is "How do you teach patience?"

It seems clear that you very well understand the personality of your older boy and his marked contrast with your second child. *Teaching* him patience isn't going to solve your problem, even if you could do it, which I doubt.

However, what he does need is someone to help him to be more successful. If you could help him to have some successes, this might motivate him to try to do better in other things. Children like your son often do their best when working alongside someone else. They are more likely to complete a project if someone else is working with them. This is not just for the actual help that the other person gives, but more for the moral support. In fact, this may be one way in which you put the "spark" into these boys—sometimes they seem to catch a little spark from the person who has it.

Is Terry this kind of boy who works best with someone else? Or is he the kind who does well starting a project and then with your help planning to finish it at some later time? If so, it is up to you to tell him that it is all right to stop now, but that he will want to come back to the thing later. Then his stopping will not be seen as a failure but part of a planned program of installment production.

Actually, it is quite typical of the Eight-year-old to make better starts than he does endings. By Nine or Ten most children are better at completing projects. So you may hope that increased age alone will bring some improvement.

However, it's quite possible that Terry won't change too much. Growth will help some, but he may always be a person who rushes through life, making his best contributions in an initial spurt and then leaving someone else to finish up the details. Consider what your son is best at. Is he a great talker, a thinker? Is he better at gross motor sports? Is he a planner and more of an executive type? Try to give him more outlets in areas in which he *can* achieve. Success at anything—it doesn't matter what—might help him to be less impatient with himself.

PREMATURE DAUGHTER, NINE,
NOT READY FOR FIFTH GRADE

Dear Dr. Ames:
My Nine-and-a-half-year-old daughter, Sandra, is about to enter fifth grade. Sandra gets fairly good grades, but I have always felt that she started school too soon (when she was only Four and a half) and has always been overplaced. The school does not agree. I feel this was especially so since Sandra was premature—only Seven-and-a-half months when she was born and weighed only three pounds. She is in a so-called open school so they say it really doesn't matter what grade she is in.

Can you advise about her placement and also recommend a book about prematurity?

I can indeed advise about her placement. Open school or closed, a Nine-and-a-half year-old girl who was a month and a half premature is not by my figuring ready for fifth grade. Your judgment as a mother is very sound here, and I would insist on a review of the situation.

The most comprehensive book we know of on the subject of prematurity is *Born Too Soon: Pre-term Birth and Early Development* by Susan Goldberg and Barbara DiVitto (Freeman Press). I can also tell you that most people now take prematurity more seriously than they used to. We used to figure that if a child seemed healthy and normal, one merely subtracted the amount of prematurity from the child's legal age and proceeded accordingly. Two months' prematurity would make a difference in your expectations during the first year or so of life—we figured—but would make relatively little by Five or Six.

Now most specialists agree that the fetus really needs those final weeks inside the mother and that many reading and perceptual and other academic problems can be related to immaturity. Don't borrow trouble, but do be alert to any signs of difficulty, as you are doing. And especially keep in mind that your daughter was not really even Four and one-half when she started kindergarten.

NOW HE GOES AROUND THE HOUSE SINGING

Dear Dr. Ames:

We were so happy and grateful to read what you had to say about grade placement. It helped my husband and me to make what we believe to be one of the most important decisions we have ever made concerning our Nine-year-old son, Dennis, for whom school has always been an unhappy place where he did not fit and didn't know why.

He was about to go into fourth grade this fall, though we knew full well he would be getting in deeper and deeper. How to help him? We prayed for an answer and then by good luck came upon your column. It hit us like a ton of bricks. This must be where the problem lay. Our boy was really overplaced in school. Not academically, but on the social behavior level—straining to the breaking point to perform beyond his degree of maturity. How had we been so blind?

So we made our decision, then secured the principal's cooperation, then our son's. We won't pretend it was entirely easy, but little did we expect to see the immediate results that came forth. After the initial shock wore off, Dennis began to go around the house *singing.* It was as though a heavy weight had been lifted from his shoulders.

We are more and more certain as the weeks go by that this will be a great school year for our son. But more than that, a great year to be alive. How much easier to show your love to a child who is on the march at his own pace than to one who is floundering and drowning before your very eyes and you don't know how to save him!

Thank you very much for your letter. I hope it may give other parents the courage to do the same thing you did.

Most people worry a great deal about the emotional damage it may do a child to repeat a grade. Few seem to worry, as you did, about the much greater danger of damage to a child's personality caused by day after day of school failure.

We grown-ups tend to take all of this rather lightly. We often act as if it's "too bad" a child gets poor grades, and we often say that he should try harder. We close our eyes, our hearts, and our minds to what it must be like to be forced day in and day out to be part of a situation that is hopelessly over one's head and in which one experiences nothing but failure.

Many of those who run our schools and who make the rules seem not to appreciate what it must be like for a child always to fail.

Let's all try to be a little more realistic and to have a little more sympathy for the boy or girl who is nowhere near ready for the school performance expected of him.

NINE-YEAR-OLD AFRAID TO RECITE

Dear Dr. Ames:

Can you help us with a very severe problem we have with our Nine-year-old daughter, Samantha? She is an attractive, bright little girl with a remarkable number of friends. She seems happy and well adjusted, and gets along very nicely with her father and with me.

She has always liked school and has always gotten good grades—but lately she has developed an extreme fear of reciting before the class. She has never liked to do this. But now in this grade the children recite and then the other children criticize their recitations.

This causes her such a panic that when she gets up to recite, all she can do is cry. This makes her very embarrassed, and lately she has begun refusing to go to school.

The teacher is very cooperative about this. She has had her erase the blackboards and do other things that will get her up before the class. These new things seem to help for a little while, but then she goes back to being afraid. And now she just doesn't want to go to school at all. What can we do to help her overcome this fear?

As your daughter gets along so well in so many ways, it does not seem as if her difficulty is, at this time, severe enough to warrant taking her to a psychologist or getting other special professional help. It may eventually come to that, but we do not think it is needed at this time.

In our opinion, the best thing to do would be to respect this extreme shyness that she feels. It is kind and cooperative of the teacher to think up these ruses, such as having her clean off the blackboard. But such efforts are not enough. Her diffidence and fear seem to be too deep-seated.

We would recommend, if the teacher is willing, just not having her recite before the class, say for the rest of the semester or better still until she asks to recite. She might be able to recite to the teacher privately if time could be arranged.

You can help her believe that later on she will have the courage and ability to recite in front of the class, as the others do. But let her know that till that time comes, you and the teacher will go along with her.

Sometimes these very shy children who cannot speak their own words in front of a classroom are able to take part in a play in which they are not themselves, but someone else. You might try this with her. It might help.

But in general when a child shows this kind of diffidence, you make the most progress by not pushing her. Rather let her go slowly and let her know that you and the teacher respect and understand her feelings. Girls like Samantha often learn by listening and watching others rather than by reciting themselves. Their intellect often outstrips their emotional development and the development of their "sense of self." Protecting such children is not coddling them—it is simply showing respect for their way of growing.

It is more important that Samantha keep going to school, and that she like school and feel comfortable there, than that she recite in front of the class.

"MUMMY, I REALLY NEED A FRIEND"

Dear Dr. Ames:

I am having an ethical problem with my daughter, Patty. Patty is Nine, a fourth-grade student. She does well with her schoolwork but it is not easy for her to make friends. I don't know exactly why, as she is a pretty little girl and we think very dear. Admittedly she is a little shy, and maybe that is the problem.

Anyway, she has finally found herself a friend, or at least the makings of one. The only trouble is that this little girl, Elaine, who sits next to her, has offered to be "best friends" if Patty will let her copy from Pat's papers. Patty didn't want to do this. She thought it was wrong. But as she put it, "Mummy, I really need a friend."

We appreciate Patty's predicament. It is no light thing for a child to need a friend (at school or elsewhere). Nobody who can remember playing alone at recess can underestimate the importance of having a friend of your own at school. We see this even at the nursery-school level.

Nor do we think that Elaine is necessarily a little monster or potentially delinquent in her demand to copy from your daughter's papers. Early lapses from a strict moral code are not unusual, even through the preteens, and especially if a child is not very good at her lessons.

We think we would advise Patty as follows. Tell her that it is indeed terribly important to have friends. Explain to her that except for the very fortunate who all through their lives seem to attract and keep plenty of them seemingly with little effort, most of us keep our friends at a certain cost.

To have friends, most children (some more slowly and with more difficulty than others) learn that they do have to make certain adaptations. At the earlier ages they have to play what the other person wants to, at least part of the time. They have to play at the other person's house sometimes, whether they want to or not. Sometimes they have to go places they don't especially want to just because their friend does want to.

But we would advise Patty that one's response to the demands of friendship must stop somewhere. In our opinion, they should stop this side of the line of any behavior that you yourself know to be wrong. Nearly any child knows that copying from other children's papers in school is wrong. Patty knows. If she gives in here, Elaine's demands will almost certainly grow stronger and stronger— the price of her friendship will become higher and higher.

If, as one may hope, Elaine is basically a nice little girl and really likes Patty, the chances are that she will be friends anyway, even without being allowed to copy. If not, Patty, though perhaps lonely, will probably be well out of this friendship.

ALLERGY MAY INDEED BE AT THE BASIS OF POOR SCHOOL FUNCTIONING

Dear Dr. Ames:

As a school psychologist and parent of a Nine-year-old who is having a lot of trouble in school, I was much interested in your recent column to the effect that allergy, unsuspected, can often lie at the basis of school difficulty. Will you write more on this subject?

I will indeed. A colleague of ours, allergist Ray Wunderlich, finds such a close relation between physical condition and learning that he believes it can go both ways. Treating a child's allergy can result in improved learning, and improvement in learning can help an allergic condition go away. Improvement in learning can also accompany improvement in coordination, vision, nutrition, or emotion.

As Dr. Wunderlich points out, a child's behavior has many causes. The reason may be physical, emotional, or a mixture of both. Child behavior can be improved in specific ways at times. Cortisonelike drugs are strong antiallergy medicines. When used in small doses they can be very effective.

He notes that

Neurologic and allergic dysfunction occur together with such regularity that one suspects on incidence factors alone that there is a relationship between the two. Often it appears that the allergic disorder is primary, with neurologic dysfunction a manifestation of the allergic process. . . . In some children, clinical treatment proof is so dramatic that there is no doubt that allergy produces neurologic dysfunction. For example, a child with hyper-activity, poor attention span, distractibility, and aggressiveness, *may become completely normal when an offending food is removed from his diet.* At the same time, his reflexes, coordination, and visual-motor performance improves. This same child may relapse when the harmful food is reintroduced into his diet, and improve again when it is withdrawn.[14]

But function and structure are closely related. As Dr. Wunderlich points out, when the neurologically handicapped child is treated with perceptual-motor training, an accompanying allergic condition may improve or disappear.

And so it can, indeed, go both ways. If you improve a child's functioning, his physical condition may improve, *or* if you improve his physical condition, his behavior may improve.

Many, many years ago Dr. Gesell pointed out that "Behavior is a function of structure." Sometimes it is hard to say where one leaves off and the other begins. But because of the close interrelationship of the two, it is always sensible, if your efforts at motivating a child and getting him to try harder and do better do not succeed, to look very closely at his body. An undiscovered allergy may indeed be at the basis of the poor school functioning of all too many boys and girls in our public schools today.

SHOULD STUDENTS BE TAUGHT ABOUT AIDS IN SEX EDUCATION CLASSES?

Dear Dr. Ames:
I am a teacher in a school system that, like most, provides courses in sex education. However, as probably always, there are major controversies—with very strong feelings on both sides—as to what should be taught when.

The current hot issue has to do with AIDS. Some feel that when children ask about it—what it is and how you get it—they should be answered truthfully. Others think not. In fact, in our district there is a rule that the subject should NOT be taught and that children's questions about it should be ignored.

What is your opinion?

That's a tough question, and whichever way the school decides some parents are going to be upset. My own feeling about sex education in school is that it should be appropriate to the age and understanding of the children being taught.

In our experience—and certainly this rule would vary with the kind of home the child comes from—most Seven-year-olds may understand that the seed (or whatever) that fertilizes the egg comes from the father. Most that we have known, however, are not too clear about the actual role the father plays. Thus even a full description of ordinary intercourse may indeed be over the heads of many second- (or perhaps even third-) graders. Needless to say, any description of variations on the customary types of intercourse would seem inappropriate.

However, our general rule for giving information about sex, whether at home or at school, is that any question asked should be answered frankly and in as much detail as one assumes the child is mature enough to understand.

Nowadays when so many radio and TV programs deal with the subject of AIDS, when the print media abound with stories about it, when even in the child's own school some child may have been excluded from classes because he or she had AIDS, it seems unrealistic to duck the subject.

What the instructor says about it will need to be carefully tailored to the maturity and presumed informational level of the students. (Hopefully most in any one class will be at more or less the same level.) For the younger grades, one need not give all possible detail.

But I don't think that one can dodge the subject entirely. Probably a good rule of thumb would be to treat the subject more or less as you would in the past have handled other social diseases. It will be tricky at best and not necessarily easy. But I don't believe that schools can avoid it entirely.

DANGER FROM STRANGERS

Dear Dr. Ames:

I appreciate the danger that children may indeed be kidnapped, abducted, or otherwise harmed by strangers, but it seems most unlikely that this could happen in our quiet town. Don't you feel that all this public emphasis on this kind of danger—having pictures of missing children in the papers and even on milk cartons—is frightening a good many children unnecessarily? Do we really need to make quite so much of all this?

In my opinion the fears that some of us are instilling in young people are extravagant and excessive. Considering that only a small portion of our children will actually be attacked or abducted, I feel that we do children more harm than good by all our warnings. The fear that we instill in them may be far worse than anything that will actually happen to most. Right?

Wrong! These things actually *could* happen in your quiet town. They could actually happen in your own family. Having fire drills in the schools does not, to my knowledge, frighten many children, and has undoubtedly saved lives in the case of real fires.

Similarly, in these very troubled times, scary or not, I believe that every parent owes it to his or her child to give that child certain warnings and to provide certain precautions. You can and should, of course, do this calmly. And unless your neighborhood seems particularly dangerous to you—or you have an ex-spouse who might indeed resort to kidnapping—you should try to present this information calmly and as if the danger was not really likely to occur. Here are a few commonsense rules and suggestions that you can reasonably offer your child without frightening him or her unduly:

1. If a stranger asks for help or directions, just say politely, "I'm sorry, I can't help you" and walk away as quickly as possible. And don't accept anything (candy, a gift) from any stranger.
2. If a stranger follows you on the street, find a safe place as quickly as you can. Look out for a block mother's home. Or go to a store or a gas station and tell an adult that you think you are being followed. Never be embarrassed to ask for help.
3. If a stranger bothers you in any way, don't hesitate to run away. Drug addicts, drunks, and crazy people, or of course any who have unfriendly intentions can indeed be very frightening. Don't worry about being unfriendly. Just run away and ask for help. Or if you've just left school or a store, go back where you started.
4. Never get into a car with a stranger even if this person says your mother sent him or her to bring you home.
5. If by any chance (and this would be more apt to happen in the city than in a small town) somebody tries to take your lunch money or some of your possessions, it is better to give up whatever it is than to struggle.
6. Keep as safe a distance as you can from other people when on the street or in a bus or subway. If you notice someone getting too close, try to move away.
7. Try to look busy. Even if you are afraid, try to look as if you know what you are doing. But avoid staring at people or looking them in the eye.
8. When you are on the street, always pay attention to what is happening around you. Don't get so involved with your friends that you don't pay attention to other people.

However, despite all your precautions, some children are going to get mugged or even sexually assaulted. What to do then? Parents may wish to try the following:

1. Check, first of all, for physical injury. Give your child all the reassurance you can muster. Try to keep or seem reasonably calm.
2. Make sure that your child is certain that the incident was not his fault.
3. As time goes on, watch for symptoms that your child may continue to worry about the experience. Symptoms to watch for include sleeplessness, loss of appetite, and depression. If your child is unable to forget what happened, seek professional help.
4. Do not become overprotective but do take what steps you can to avoid a repetition of the incident, as trying to make sure that your child doesn't walk alone.
5. Discuss with him ways to get help if need be, or to stay safe. You might even consider enrolling him in a self-defense class if your neighborhood is unusually unsafe. (Some people favor this; some do not.)
6. If the threat is constant, perhaps you can work with other parents to provide a safety system, such as parent patrols or group activities, that will keep your child off the street unless he absolutely needs to be there.

It is hard to have to face up to these problems. When I was growing up about the worst that happened to a child was that some other child would say mean things to him. The world is more dangerous now. So even at the risk of possibly frightening your child, you do owe it to him to plan what he could do if some really dangerous incident should take place.

SHOULD NINE-YEAR-OLD GIRL BE TOLD
WHO HER REAL MOTHER IS?

Dear Dr. Ames:
When I was seventeen I gave birth to a baby girl who is now Nine years old. I was not married and was advised to give the baby up for adoption. However, due to a

physical defect she was not considered adoptable so I took her home, as I had wanted to from the beginning.

My parents were wonderful enough to accept her in their home. My mother took care of her while I worked. From the start I wanted to raise her as my own. Although my mother was wonderful, she quietly undermined my efforts to be the child's mother.

So when I realized that Angie might be getting confused, I backed down and let my mother take the reins. Angie now thinks that my parents are her parents.

I am now married and my husband has been very understanding about the whole thing. My daughter seems to be normal and well adjusted, gets on well in school, has nice friends.

My husband and I wonder if she should be told about me. Recently, for instance, she needed her baptism paper to give to Sunday School. She wanted to know why she was baptized in the hospital. I said because they had a church there. We're afraid that other questions will arise later and don't know what we should do.

This of course is not specifically a Nine-year-old problem. It could pertain to a child of any age, and it is a very hard problem—especially since you say you live very near your mother and Angie.

It seems simpler to go on as you are, not telling her, and taking every precaution to keep her from finding out, until she is considerably older. However, later on—say when she is in her late teens or early twenties—it might be best for her to know the truth. Certainly before she marries. Many children seem curiously able to take this kind of information as they grow older.

You seem to have made a very good arrangement. You were fortunate that your family was willing to help out as they did. For the time being we would try not to make an issue and to see, if possible, that no issue arises.

Even now at Nine years of age, if Angie should discover

the true story of her birth, and you did have to explain things to her, we believe she would be able to accept the truth. But we wouldn't bring it up now unless you have to.

THERE ARE STILL NICE YOUNG PEOPLE

Dear Dr. Ames:

I realize that complaining to you is not going to get me anywhere. But as a grandmother, I can't help bemoaning the fact that children seem to get rougher and tougher every year—less and less friendly to older people, less and less respectful. Will things never go back to what they were?

They won't go back, and admittedly many children are less respectful to adults than in times past. But there are still so very many tremendously nice young people out there. For example, a Nine-year-old boy whom we were examining recently, when asked the routine question why in a shipwreck women and children should be rescued before men, replied, "Because the children haven't had their life yet and the women are precious because they can have babies." And we know many more just like him!

APPENDIXES
appendix a
BOOKS FOR NINE-YEAR-OLDS

Adair, Gilbert. ALICE THROUGH THE NEEDLE'S EYE. New York: Dutton, 1984.

Aiken, Joan. UP THE CHIMNEY DOWN. New York: Harper & Row, 1985.

Allard, Harry. MISS NELSON HAS A FIELD DAY. Boston: Houghton Mifflin, 1985.

Andersen, Hans Christian. THE SNOW QUEEN. Translated by Eve Le Gallienne. New York: Harper & Row, 1985.

Bagnold, Enid. NATIONAL VELVET. New York: William Morrow, 1985.

Baum, L. Frank. THE MARVELLOUS LAND OF OZ. New York: William Morrow, 1985.

Berman, Claire G. WHAT AM I DOING IN A STEPFAMILY? New York: Lyle Stuart, 1982.

Brenner, Barbara. WAGON WHEELS. New York: Harper & Row/I Can Read Book, 1978.

Brooks, Walter R. FREDDY THE PIG BOOKS (series). New York: Alfred A. Knopf, 1986.

Brown, Heywood. THE FIFTY-FIRST DRAGON. Englewood Cliffs, NJ: Prentice-Hall, 1968.

Caines, Jeanette. CHILLY STOMACH. New York: Harper & Row, 1986.

Cameron, Ann. MORE STORIES JULIAN TELLS. New York: Alfred A. Knopf, 1986.

Christian, Mary Bount. MERGER ON THE ORIENT EXPRESSWAY. New York: Dutton, 1986.

Cleary, Beverly. RAMONA THE BRAVE. New York: Yearling Books/Dell, 1975.

Cohn, Janice. I HAD A FRIEND NAMED PETER. New York: William Morrow, 1987.

Cole, Babette. THE SLIMY BOOK. New York: Random House, 1986.

Cunningham, Julia. GAF. New York: Alfred A. Knopf, 1986.

Dahl, Roald. FANTASTIC MR. FOX. New York: Alfred A. Knopf, 1970 (reprinted 1986).

Estes, Rose. THE MYSTERY OF THE TURKISH TATTOO. New York: Random House, 1986.

Fleischman, Paul. I AM PHOENIX: POEMS FOR TWO VOICES. New York: Harper & Row, 1985.

Gerstein, Mordicai. TALES OF PAN. New York: Harper & Row, 1986.

Gibbons, Gail. LIGHTS! CAMERA! ACTION! HOW A MOVIE IS MADE. New York: Crowell Junior Books, 1985.

Grollman, Earl A. TALKING ABOUT DEATH: A DIALOGUE BETWEEN PARENT AND CHILD (new ed.) Boston: Beacon Press, 1976.

Hass, E. A. INCOGNITO MOSQUITO TAKES TO THE AIR. New York: Random House, 1986.

Hastings, Selina. SIR GAWAIN AND THE LOATHLY LADY. New York: Lothrop, Lee & Shepard, 1985.

Herriot, James. ONLY ONE WOOF. New York: St. Martin's Press, 1985.

Holmes, Barbara Ware. CHARLOTTE CHEETHAM: MASTER OF DISASTER. New York: Harper & Row, 1986.

Hughes, Frieda. GETTING RID OF AUNT EDNA. New York: Harper & Row, 1986.

Hughes, Shirley. CHIPS AND JESSIE. New York: Lothrop, Lee & Shepard, 1986.

Irving, Washington. RIP VAN WINKLE. New York: Books of Wonder/William Morrow, 1987.

Johnson, Ginny, and Clutchins, Judy. ANDY BEAR: A POLAR

Bear Cub Grows Up at the Zoo. New York: William Morrow, 1985.

Jones, Rebecca C. Germy Blew It. New York: Dutton, 1987.

Kallow, Robert, and Kallow, Linda. A Few Thousand of the Best Free Things in America (a catalogue). Yonkers, NY: Roblin Press, 1983.

Keller, Charles. Astronauts: Space Jokes and Riddles. Englewood Cliffs, NJ: Prentice-Hall, 1985.

Kessler, Leonard. The Worst Team Ever. New York: Greenwillow, 1985.

Kipling, Rudyard. Just So Stories. New York: Doubleday, 1946.

Kitchner, Margaret. Grandmother Goes Up the Mountain. New York: Dutton, 1986.

Lexau, Joan. The Homework Caper. New York: Harper & Row, 1985.

Lionni, Leo. Frederick's Fables: A Treasury of Favorite Stories. New York: Pantheon, 1985.

Mannes, Stephen. Chicken Trek. New York: Dutton, 1987.

Mayle, Peter. Where Did I Come From? New York: Lyle Stuart, 1973.

Mebs, Gudrun. Sunday's Child. New York: Dutton, 1986.

Nimo, Jenny. The Snow Spider. New York: Dutton, 1987.

Park, Barbara. The Kid in the Red Jacket. New York: Alfred A. Knopf, 1987.

Powzyk, Joyce. Wallaby Creek. New York: Lothrop, Lee & Shepard, 1985.

Parish, Peggy. Merry Christmas, Amelia Bedelia. New York: Greenwillow, 1986.

Randolph, John. Backpacking Basics. Englewood Cliffs, NJ: Prentice-Hall, 1982.

Roos, Stephen. The Terrible Truth. New York: Delacorte, 1983.

Rosen, Michael. Don't Put Mustard in the Custard. New York: Dutton, 1986.

Schultz, Charles M. Snoopy's Getting Married. New York: Random House, 1986.

Seixas, Judith. DRUGS: WHAT THEY ARE, WHAT THEY DO. New York: Greenwillow, 1987.

Shreve, Susan. HOW I SAVED THE WORLD ON PURPOSE. New York: Holt, Rinehart & Winston, 1985.

Silverstein, Shel. THE GIVING TREE. New York: Harper & Row, 1964.

Simon, Seymour. THE DINOSAUR IS THE BIGGEST ANIMAL THAT EVER LIVED. New York: Lippincott, 1984.

————. BITS AND BYTES: A COMPUTER DICTIONARY FOR BEGINNERS. New York: Crowell Junior Books, 1985.

Singer, Marilyn. LIZZIE SILVER OF SHERWOOD FOREST. New York: Harper & Row, 1986.

Slate, Alfred. THE TROUBLE ON JANUS. New York: Lippincott Junior Books, 1985.

Stevenson, James. WHEN I WAS NINE. New York: Greenwillow, 1986.

Stine, Megan, and Stine, H. William. THE SPEAR OF AZZURRA. New York: Random House, 1986.

Sullivan, George. PITCHER. New York: Crowell Junior Books, 1986.

Taylor, Mildred D. THE GOLD CADILLAC. New York: Dutton, 1987.

Weiss, Nicki. IF YOU'RE HAPPY AND YOU KNOW IT. EIGHTEEN STORY SONGS SET TO PICTURES. New York: Greenwillow, 1987.

appendix b
BOOKS FOR PARENTS OF NINE-YEAR-OLDS

Ames, Louise Bates. Is Your Child in the Wrong Grade? Rosemont, NJ: Modern Learning Press, 1978.

———. What Am I Doing in This Grade? Rosemont, NJ: Programs for Education, 1985.

———. Straight Answers to Parents Questions. New York: Clarkson N. Potter, 1988.

Ames, Louise Bates, and Haber, Carol Chase. He Hit Me First. New York: Dembner, 1982.

———. Your Eight-Year-Old: Lively and Outgoing. New York: Delacorte, 1989.

Armstrong, Thomas. In Their Own Way. New York: Jeremy P. Tarcher/St. Martin's Press, 1987.

Berman, Claire. What Am I Doing in a Stepfamily? New York: Lyle Stuart, 1982.

Calladine, Andrew, and Calladine, Carole. One Terrific Year: Supporting Your Kids Through the Ups and Downs of Their Year. Minneapolis, MN: Winston Press, 1985.

Comer, James P., and Pouissaint, Alvin F. Black Child Care: How to Bring Up a Healthy Black Child in America. New York: Pocket Books, 1980.

Crook, William G. Tracking Down Hidden Food Allergy. Jackson, TN: Professional Books, 1980.

Crook, William G., and Stevens, Laura J. Solving the Puzzle of Your Hard-to-Raise Child. New York: Random House, 1988.

Dodson, Fitzhugh. How to Parent. New York: New American Library, 1973.

———. How to Discipline with Love. New York: Rawson, 1978.

———. How to Single Parent. New York: Harper & Row, 1988.

Feingold, Ben. Why Your Child Is Hyperactive. New York: Random House, 1974.

Ferber, Richard. "The Child Who Doesn't Sleep." In Schiff, Eileen, ed., Experts Advise Parents. New York: Delacorte, 1987.

Forer, Lucille, The Birth Order Factor. New York: McKay, 1976.

Galland, Leo. Superimmunity for Kids. New York: Dutton, 1988.

Gardner, Howard. Frames of Mind. New York: Basic Books, 1983.

Gesell, Arnold; Ilg, Frances L.; and Ames, Louise B. The Child from Five to Ten (rev. ed.). New York: Harper & Row, 1977.

Goldstein, Sonja, and Solnit, Albert. Divorce and Your Child: Practical Suggestions for Parents. New Haven, CT: Yale University Press, 1984.

Grant, Jim. I Hate School. Rosemont, NJ: Programs for Education, 1986.

Grollman, Earl A., and Sweder, Gerri. The Working Parent Dilemma: How to Balance the Responsibility of Children and Career. Boston: Beacon Press, 1986.

Healy, Jane M. Your Child's Growing Mind. New York: Doubleday, 1987.

Ilg, Frances L.; Ames, Louise Bates; and Baker, Sidney M. Child Behavior (rev. ed.). New York: Harper & Row, 1981.

Kramer, Rita. In Defense of the Family: Raising Children in America Today. New York: Basic Books, 1983.

Lerman, Saf. Parent Awareness Training: Positive Parenting for the 1980s. New York: A & W Publishers, 1980.

McGuinness, Diane. WHEN CHILDREN DON'T LEARN: UNDERSTANDING THE BIOLOGY AND PSYCHOLOGY OF LEARNING DISABILITIES. New York: Basic Books, 1985.

Matthews, Sanford J., and Brinley, Maryann B. THROUGH THE MOTHERHOOD MAZE. New York: Doubleday, 1982.

Melina, Lois. RAISING ADOPTED CHILDREN. New York: Solstice Press/Harper & Row, 1986.

Moore, Sheila, and Frost, Roon. THE LITTLE BOY BOOK. New York: Clarkson & Potter, 1986.

Packard, Vance. OUR ENDANGERED CHILDREN: GROWING UP IN A CHANGING WORLD. Boston: Little, Brown, 1983.

Pitcher, Evelyn Goodenough, and Schultz, Lynn Hickey. BOYS AND GIRLS AT PLAY: THE DEVELOPMENT OF SEX ROLES. South Hadley, MA: Bergin & Garvey, 1983.

Procaccini, Joseph, and Kiefaber, Mark W. P.L.U.S. PARENTING: TAKE CHARGE OF YOUR FAMILY. New York: Doubleday, 1985.

Rapp, Doris J. ALLERGIES AND THE HYPERACTIVE CHILD. New York: Sovereign Books/Simon & Schuster, 1980.

Scarr, Sandra. MOTHER CARE OTHER CARE. New York: Basic Books, 1984.

Schaefer, Charles. HOW TO INFLUENCE CHILDREN: A COMPLETE GUIDE TO BECOMING A BETTER PARENT. New York: Van Nostrand Reinhold, 1982.

Schiff, Eileen, ed. EXPERTS ADVISE PARENTS. New York: Delacorte, 1987.

Smith, Lendon. FEED YOUR KIDS RIGHT. New York: McGraw-Hill, 1979.

Smith, Sally L. NO EASY ANSWERS: TEACHING THE LEARNING DISABLED CHILD. Boston: Little, Brown, 1979.

Stein, Sara Bonnett. GIRLS AND BOYS: THE LIMITS OF NONSEXIST CHILD RAISING. New York: Scribners, 1985.

Stevens, Laura J.; Stevens, George E.; and Stoner, Rosemary G. HOW TO FEED YOUR HYPERACTIVE CHILD. New York: Doubleday, 1972.

Trelease, Jim. THE READ-ALOUD HARDBOOK. New York: Penguin, 1985.

Vail, Priscilla L. THE WORLD OF THE GIFTED CHILD. New York: Walker, 1985.

————. SMART KIDS WITH SCHOOL PROBLEMS. New York: Dutton, 1987.

Visher, Emily, and Visher, John. HOW TO WIN AS A STEPFAMILY. New York: Scribner/Norton, 1982.

Wunderlich, Ray C., and Kalita, Dwight K. NOURISHING YOUR CHILD. New Canaan, CT: Keats, 1984.

NOTES

1. Described in Healy, Jane M. YOUR CHILD'S GROWING MIND. New York: Doubleday, 1987, p. 75.
2. Procaccini, Joseph, and Kiefaber, Mark W. P.L.U.S. PARENTING: TAKE CHARGE OF YOUR FAMILY. New York: Doubleday, 1985, pp. 200–205
3. Ibid., p. 200.
4. Ibid., pp. 203–204.
5. Ibid., p. 205.
6. Gesell, Arnold; Ilg, Frances L.; and Ames, Louise B. THE CHILD FROM FIVE TO TEN (rev. ed.). New York: Harper & Row, 1977, p. 193.
7. National Assessment of Educational Progress. Denver, CO
8. Healy, YOUR CHILD'S GROWING MIND, pp. 82–83.
9. Grant, Jim. I HATE SCHOOL. Rosemont, NJ: Programs for Education, 1986, p. 42.
10. Vail, Priscilla. THE WORLD OF THE GIFTED CHILD. New York: Walker, 1985, pp. 81, 85.
11. Ibid.
12. Packard, Vance. OUR ENDANGERED CHILDREN: GROWING UP IN A CHANGING WORLD. Boston: Little, Brown, 1983.
13. Crook, William G., and Stevens, Laura J. SOLVING THE PUZZLE OF YOUR HARD-TO-RAISE CHILD. New York: Random House, 1988, p. 94.
14. Wunderlich, Ray C., and Kalita, Dwight K. NOURISHING YOUR CHILD. New Canaan, CT: Keats, 1984.

INDEX